MY DWELLING PLACE

A PLACE OF SURRENDER

GLENDA VAUGHN

WESTBOW PRESS®
A DIVISION OF THOMAS NELSON
& ZONDERVAN

WestBow Press books may be ordered through booksellers or by contacting:

WestBow Press
A Division of Thomas Nelson & Zondervan
1663 Liberty Drive
Bloomington, IN 47403
www.westbowpress.com
1 (866) 928-1240

ISBN: 978-1-5127-1507-1 (sc)
ISBN: 978-1-5127-1508-8 (e)

Library of Congress Control Number: 2015916373

Print information available on the last page.

WestBow Press rev. date: 10/26/2015

DEDICATION

I am thankful to all of my family and friends
for their love and encouragement through the
years. Through them and Jesus my hope was
renewed. This book is dedicated to my children
and to the memory of my precious Mother,
Velvia Kelly Bates.

Glenda Vaughn

It is surprising to me that my journaling has turned into a book and through these pages I hope to express my thankfulness to God for all that He has brought me through. Without His never ending Love, beautiful Grace and continuing Mercy I would not have survived some of my life experiences. My Joy is in His Strength! I want to encourage you to get to know Him intimately. Spend time in His Presence. Know Him as Friend, Companion, Father and honor Him as Lord, Master and King.

Glenda Vaughn

CONTENTS

The following words found their way into my heart and came out in song as I sought a way to honor my wonderful Jesus.

MY DWELLING PLACE

Gods' Love Surrounds Me I Feel His
Holy Presence Everywhere
Each Breath I Breathe Exclaims His
Grace, Mercy and Loving Care.
As I Start Out Each New Day He Enters When
I Praise Him, Mighty King of Kings
At His Feet And On My Face I Find My Dwelling Place.

Chorus

I Find My Dwelling Place At The Feet
Of Jesus, His Holy Grace.
His Majesty Will Reign Within My Heart Forevermore.
When Life's Race Is Finally Through
Fathers Love Will Take Me To
The Home My Soul Is Longing For, My Dwelling Place.

Holy Spirit Tells Me The Path That
I Must Follow Everyday
Surrendering My Will, Let His
Spirit Fill, Walk In His Way

Resting In Gods' Love, Free As A Mourning
Dove I Give My Life To Him
At His Feet And On My Face I Find My Dwelling Place

Chorus

I Found My Dwelling Place At The
Feet Of Jesus, His Holy Grace
His Majesty Will Reign Within My Heart Forevermore
When Life's Work On Earth Is Through
Fathers' Love Will Take Me To
The Home My Soul Is Longing For My Dwelling Place
At His Feet And On My Face I Found My Dwelling Place.

© 1999 GLENDA VAUGHN 2015 OUR
DESTINY MUSIC PUBLISHING BMI

Expressing my love to my heavenly Father was not always my priority. I gave my heart to Jesus at age five but came to be baptized at age four-teen in a revival service and was "saved" by all my Pastors accounts. I admit that I have given almighty God many reasons to want to throw me back into the cesspool of earthly life, but for His Grace go I.

Sanctification has been a long, drawn out continuing process and I will be the first to admit that I am still a work in progress. I do realize though that Gods' love and mercy has kept me through years of tears and valleys of indecision and procrastination. I've had a very stubborn will and it has been tested and tried again and again. The hardest thing that I've ever done is to let God be God. I am somewhat better than I used to be. Sometimes I wonder if Heavenly Father is just shaking His head and wondering WHY did I make this one? I can imagine that because I know He must have a sense of humor.

Dying to self is harder for some than others. My self-will has had to be broken a little at a time. I used to plan every area of my life and hope that it met with God's approval. Not releasing my will has caused me much heartache. Scripture says stubbornness is rebellion.

NIV (1 John 3:4) Everyone who sins breaks the law. In fact sin is lawlessness.

When we think of sin we may want to put each one in different categories as if one was more sinful than another. Sometimes we think that "a little sin" is ok. Sin is sin. However, the Commandments are a different matter and we should know and obey them. We need to stay prayed up so that there is no sin between us and God. Thankfully, He is still a God of forgiveness.

Sin is disobedience to Gods law. When we choose our will over God's will it is sin. Our self-centered attitude and our pride are the root cause of rebellion to Holy God, Jehovah. We want our own way.

NIV (Jeremiah 5: 23) But these people have stubborn and rebellious hearts. They have turned aside and gone

We should not continue in the same sin if we have truly been saved because His seed of righteousness has been planted in our hearts and He will draw us back to Himself. We all sin daily though and Holy Spirit will continue to remind us of who we belong to.

NIV (Psalms 91:1-2) He who dwells in the shelter of the Most High will rest in the shadow of the Almighty. I will say of the Lord, He is my refuge and my fortress, my God, in whom I trust.

This verse so clearly shows us that if we make Him Lord of our lives then we can rightfully call Him Master. We will enjoy the protection and provision that being under His authority allows to us.

So many years were wasted taking almighty God for granted. I called on Him when I was desperate and ignored Him between emergencies. With all that I've done the God of the universe still loves me. He still answers my prayers. He allows his grace to keep me and has healed my family and me in times of sickness. There are times that He provides things for me before I even ask. Often I will have something on my mind and it will be provided without my asking. His love is more awesome than my words can express. His presence is quiet, peaceful and comforting. In His presence I find my well, drinking from his wisdom, trusting in His goodness. At his feet and on my face I continue to find my dwelling place.

FOCUS ON THE FATHER

I've had to learn gradually to get my mind off the circumstances of my life and focus on God as Father. He has been patient and kind and has been the kind of Father that we all wish we had in our earthly fathers. My dad was not around that much growing up. He worked out of town much of the time and when he was home he was usually partying with his friends. Most of life's early lessons were taught by my Mother. She was a dyed in the white wool of The Lamb, Christian lady. She believed in the Son of God with every fiber of her being. She was a quiet, humble woman but her kind spirit was never mistaken for weakness. She spent much time alone and sacrificed in every way while rearing eight children. With all the challenges she went through her faith was taught on her knees.

One of my brothers was crippled from birth. He never spoke and she spent many nights with no sleep as he suffered through sometimes ten seizures a night. He went to Heaven when he was eight-teen years of age. With all that she experienced I never heard my mother complain. When I got older I asked her many times how she could go on. Her response was always the same. We were to serve the Lord and be content in whatever state we found ourselves. That was not a pious attitude. She believed and lived her life that way, always making the best of every situation.

Obviously, I checked out on that virtue lesson as well as many others. I find myself complaining when I have no reason compared to so many. One of my most precious memories at home was hearing my Mama pray out loud every night as she asked Gods' blessing on each of us by name. When I woke in the morning to a hot breakfast and warm house she was usually singing gospel hymns as she did her daily chores.

She focused on the Father.

When I was growing up there was never any question of whether we were going to church. If the doors were open we were there. We lived on a country road and attended the church about a mile down the same road. Usually we walked. The sheer joy of being outside in the sunshine, singing as we walked, is a wonderful memory. We were scrubbed and in our Sunday best which sometimes meant white gloves. This of course was perfect attire for catching tadpoles in the mud holes on either side of the road, a country child's heaven. I spent more than a few Sundays getting a second wash off before going into service. My Mamas' Irish temper during those times usually turned into laughter before we were done. God sure picked the right Mom for us. She was the ideal Proverbs 31 woman. Her character was modeled after her heavenly father. Though I may never be the example that my mother was, like her, I've had to learn to get my mind off the circumstances of life. God has taught me that His way is not always to remove my problems but to give me His strength in coping with them. Usually kicking and screaming but ultimately, He allows me the grace to surrender them to Him. I could save so much energy and time if I would just give them to Him first.

NIV (Matthew 11:28-30) says; "Come to me all you who are weary and burdened and I will give you rest. Take My yoke upon you and learn from Me, for I am gentle and humble in heart, and you will find rest for your souls. For My yoke is easy and My burden is light." That is the scripture that always comes to my mind. It is the one that I heard as I gave my heart to Jesus.

God is more interested in building our character than in changing our circumstances. We have all heard this but I know that it is true. For some of us it takes a little more persuasion. If we call ourselves Christians we must commit to having the character of Christ. To have his character we have to accept that we have the mind of

Christ. If we are in Him and He is in us we can trust that we have the mind of Christ. If we are walking in His will we will know how to make the decisions we need to make. We have to surrender to Him in every area of our life.

Also, we must know His nature. The Bible is our character reference and Holy Spirit reveals the nature of Christ.

We all hear the call of God differently. His divine nature is in all of us and if we want to hear we will recognize His call. He sees in us potential that we are not even aware of. Often we are dumfounded when we hear of a particular call on someone we know. We might never have recognized that ability and talent in that person. They may never see in us the potential that God sees either. That is not the only matter however.

A strong, intimate relationship is imperative and is the cornerstone of being able to know beyond a doubt that it is Gods' voice we are hearing. We have to believe and obey the precepts that God has laid out for us. Our character is built by the decisions that we make day by day. We must know that as a child of God we can ask for His guidance in every situation and be assured that He will lead us in the right way.

Sometimes I still hear the question when a decision is to be made. What would Jesus do? That is a good guideline to remind us to take even the smallest decisions to Him.

As we progress in our Christian walk there are some basic principles and simple teachings that may be helpful. Especially new converts may question from time to time whether they are truly saved even though they have gone through doctrinal teaching and acceptance of Christ as their Savior. Satan tries to make us doubt so we will give up before we are strong enough to build our faith.

NIV (1 John 3:16) "For God so loved the world that He gave His one and only Son that whoever believes in Him shall not perish but have eternal life."

Settle it. Believe and follow Him. Take God at His word. Either we believe Him or we don't. Don't let the accuser steal your peace and future. (Revelations 12:10) Satan is called the accuser of the brethren. Don't let your emotions rule you. Trust what God tells you in His word and what Holy Spirit reveals to you. Many mistake emotion for anointing and let emotions rule and guide them. That may sound harsh but you need to know the difference. Legalism is so prevalent in many churches that those worldly ideas leave little room for Holy Spirit to work.

By that I mean there are so many rules and regulations according to mans' ideas on how to act, what or what not to wear, etc. This is not a play to be performed. Meeting in church is for worship and our exhortation. Some try to interpret Gods' word without the guidance of Holy Spirit and take away Gods' reverence by concentrating on their own ideas. We can and often do hurt people with such nonsense. Let Holy Spirit have His way and if any changes are to be made He knows what to say to people. The lost world needs committed Christian soldiers armed with Spiritual Armor who know the WORD and have the Anointing to free them from all the bondages that Satan has to offer. Souls need to be rescued, delivered, healed and made ready to take up their own weapons against the darkness of Satan. We have to carry out the commission that we've been entrusted with. To do this we have to be true to God and seek holiness. As we strive to know God personally, intimately we will learn how to rescue the perishing from eternal torment and free the ones that are captive by Satan's lies and deceptions by helping them know truth.

Every Christian experience is subjective. We are all on different levels of spiritual maturity. It is all dependent on our life experiences and faithfulness to the calling to lead a holy life. God is all powerful, ever present when we call on Him and all knowing. He is my El Shaddai, God Almighty! We can never live a fulfilled life unless we surrender it all to the Lord and let Him live through us. We won't worry if we are good enough then because His life will shine through us and He will be recognized in us. He will light up our lives.

FINDING MY TRUE FATHER

As Christians we all know that the Trinity is comprised of God the Father, Son Jesus and Holy Spirit. Even Non-Christians are often aware of them though they don't know them. That was the case when I was a child.

Our Mom took us to church faithfully. I was aware of God who I thought would zap me at any time because He could. That was before I knew Him well. Later I learned about Jesus in Sunday school and I grew to love Him. Holy Spirit was rarely mentioned and when He was He was referred to as the Holy Ghost. As a child I didn't want to know any ghost holy or otherwise. There definitely was a sense of fear.

When the shouting began in a good old summer, Southern revival service and THE HOLY GHOST was brought up I usually found my way outside to catch lightening bugs. If it happened to be a day service which we had often then I managed to escape to the caves and bluffs behind the church. There I found a few comrades and we would look for Indian arrowheads. My collection was abundant. Cold fresh water was always flowing from the rocks and fresh water springs. Looking back I realize that Holy Spirit was with me for years before I recognized, acknowledged and sought Him. As a small child in Sunday school my teacher told me about Jesus and how to ask him into my heart. He was very real to me and became my best friend. I talked to him often even during my childhood escapades. He was always there. I'm sure angels were always on alert. When I was in first grade on the first day of school He didn't protect me from getting a paddling on my behind. Wooden rulers hurt but it hurt my pride more. My only action for punishment was running to the window to hear the school band as they practiced their routine.

However, He protected me from being run over by the school bus when I was in first grade. Lying on the road before school I wanted to see if the big yellow bus would go over me without touching me. Also, I really didn't want to go to school that day. I've wondered many times why my older sisters and brother were not looking out for me. Hmmm ! They would never have intentionally let me be hurt but I do like to tease them. As the bus pulled away I realized that I had a day off from school. It was hooray until I met my mother at the front door telling her only that I had missed the bus. She had seen the whole thing and was powerless to stop the bus or get to me. Lucky for me I was a tiny child. She was especially nice to me that day. I didn't understand not getting punished until I had children of my own. There is nothing as strong as a mothers' love except for a fathers love especially Heavenly Father.

I know that I was protected again when I was about eight years old. My friend and I decided to sail down the small creek in the woods behind his house though we couldn't swim. There were many other times that I was in His watch care and kept from harm and didn't even realize it at the time..

When I was four-teen I was water baptized. I was last in line following my sister and our friend just in case they drowned. My faith had not yet grown.

Even through my fear of the cold water I was overwhelmed with Holy Spirit. Joy truly filled my soul and prayer became an integral part of my life. I had never been taught to know Holy Spirit so I wasn't aware that He was responsible for the unknown language that tickled my tongue and came from my mouth in spurts. I thought that somehow I had made up this exciting language that took me over when I prayed. Goose bumps covered me and joy and peace washed over me. This was strange behavior for a Southern Missionary Baptist girl. Who knew? I had found my first love and nothing would satisfy for long or so I thought.

My high school friend became very special to me. We dated until he moved away to go to college. I made plans to follow my dreams and more often than not they did not allow much time for the Lord. The world was calling and its voice was much louder than the still small voice inside. There was much to be learned and my quest for life and desire to be involved in the music business took me out of my small town and away from any hint of holiness.

My naive outlook put me on a bus headed to Atlanta, Georgia one day after high school was over. My plan was to stay in Atlanta for the summer and then go to New York. That was a big dream for a small town girl with no experience. My mama had told me not to trust anyone but the bus driver. As I arrived in Atlanta, my innocence fairly intact, the bus driver, twice my age asked me to have dinner with him. Would Mama be surprised ! My cousin had accompanied me because we were to be roommates. I declined the invitation and went with her instead. I could tell already that Atlanta was going to be FUN ! After exploring the city and settling in a job I found that I prayed less and less. Jesus, my best friend was laid aside like a used possession. I was headed for a rude awakening thinking that I could handle everything on my own.

DIOBEDIENCE EQUALS DISCIPLINE

Soon I was homesick, lonely and knowing that things would never be the same. I began a whirlwind romance and married knowing that Holy Spirit was almost shouting no. Yes, I heard Him then though I didn't want to.

NIV (Proverbs 8: 33) "Listen to my instruction and be wise. Do not ignore it."

I believe the Lord uses specific scripture to speak to us in each circumstance of life if we will hear. Even if the overall text has another application He will bring scripture to mind. Obviously I thought that I was in control and did not listen. My first error was disobedience. My second was marrying a non - Christian. I could see that basically he was a good man and he truly seemed to love me. What I didn't know was all the neglect, hurt and abuse that he was bringing into this marriage. Eventually these things must be dealt with in any relationship. Mine was no exception but I was not equipped. Life's hardest lessons were beginning that year. Six weeks into my marriage I saw a side of my husband that I didn't know existed. I relate these things not out of disrespect for him but to explain how a wounded spirit and abuse can torture a soul and turn one into an abuser. His life had been filled with emotional pain that had never been admitted, dealt with or healed.

My opinion in retrospect is that he had tried to be all things to all people and had been taken advantage of and used repeatedly. Each experience and relationship that hurt him had been layered on top of the ones before. I went into the marriage with the teaching that he was supposed to be head of the household and take care of me. According to my understanding of scripture that is true. However women have responsibilities as well. I was no more prepared to be an equal partner in the marriage than he was. He had no biblical teaching or example for a happy, successful marriage. I expected him to supply all my emotional needs as well as everything else. It wasn't fair but fair doesn't always equate in a marriage.

My immaturity, coupled with his emotional scars, were more than we could cope with. He would act out his frustrations and I would react to his treatment. It was a vicious cycle. He would hurt me then be overwhelmed with sorrow and remorse. Over and over he would promise that it would never happen again. I wanted so desperately to believe him that I forgave over and again. I made excuses for his behavior. There was always a next time. I was trying to weigh the situation from a biblical standpoint and forgive as many times as needed.

I was too young and inexperienced to realize the severity of the problem. My advice to anyone that is considering marriage is to get to know your partner as well as possible before you take your vows. I took my marriage covenant very seriously and never considered divorce those first few years. In my early years divorce did happen with some couples of course but was uncommon in my region and with my upbringing. It was not unheard of but rare. I had lived in a protected bubble in the midst of the Bible belt. I am thankful though for having been raised with strong values and a sense of family.

As we struggled to hang on to a disastrous union I became introverted and embarrassed. I thought that I could handle my problems on my own. I did not want anyone to know. The few that did know never knew the severity of it all. Day by day I was slipping into despair. In the worst times I called on God to show me what to do. At other times I blamed Him for allowing it. In the midst of it all one scripture was repeated over and over in my mind. It sounded until I grasped the meaning.

(Philippians 4:13) "I can do all things through Christ who strengthens me".

These words became my strength and my lifeline. When I discovered that I was pregnant six weeks into the marriage the doctor found a lump in my breast. During that time it was like a death sentence. I was sent to a specialist who informed me that I must make a radical decision. I could have the mass removed then and destroy my baby or wait until half way through the pregnancy and gamble with cancer. Of course there was no question. I would not sacrifice my baby. The thought of cancer terrified me. I had watched as an uncle suffered and died with cancer when I was a child. It was a horrible memory. I was anxious to seek the comfort of the Father. As I read His word calmness surrounded me.

KJV (Philippians 4 :7) "And the peace of God, which passeth all understanding shall keep your hearts and minds through Christ Jesus."

Faith flowed in and I knew my baby and I would be just fine. My husband was very loving, gentle and kind during this period. He did everything that he could to make things good. Finally, I thought our life together was going to be alright.

When our daughter was born he was the most loving dad anyone could ask for. She was like a little doll. He doted on her constantly, feeding, bathing and changing her. As she grew he took her with him almost every time he went anywhere without me. He was so proud to show her off.

When she was eight-teen months old she became very ill and had to have surgery. She had developed kidney problems a few months before but the treatments had not cured her. She had surgery and healed fine. Once again I knew that God had brought us through.

KJV (Philippians 4: 6) "Be careful for nothing but in everything by prayer and supplication with thanksgiving let your requests be made known unto God. "

I had found a small church that I attended with my sister-in-law who lived a few miles away though the church was of little comfort. They had problems that had begun before we started there and soon disbanded and closed the church. My only brother and his family were the few people that I knew. My sister and her daughter had moved up and shared an apartment with my cousin and me before I married but they had all moved out of state so I treasured and relied on my brother and his family. Problems at home had begun again and I was struggling again not to give up.

When my daughter turned two years old I had more tumors removed. The day after surgery I learned that my Dad had a massive stroke. He was only fifty-six. I checked out of the hospital against my doctor's orders and we headed out of state. We arrived a few hours before my Dad died. It was unexpected and a shock. After spending two weeks with my Mother I went back to Atlanta. The night I got home I had a miscarriage. Why was life so hard?

Guilt and loss set in. I blamed myself for not spending more time with my parents. I also blamed myself for having the surgery thinking that may have caused the miscarriage. The reality was that I didn't know that I was pregnant before the surgery. I dusted off my Bible and got really familiar with God during that time. I needed and relied on Him but I also questioned Him again.

I had not yet learned the lesson of surrender. I still thought that I was in control.

Don't waste precious time like I did with this notion. I think that part of me knew that God was supposed to take care of things and part of me thought that God was too big to bother. We have to remember that His love is not dependent on who we are but who He is. Since He gave His only Son to die for us what more do we need to prove His love for us?

Sometimes it takes a lot to break a stubborn spirit when you don't allow it to bend.

PICKING UP MY DREAM

After a while we moved into a new neighborhood and my husbands' abusive behavior escalated. He was jealous of everyone I spoke to it seemed. There was little contact with anyone except him. Eventually I made friends with the neighbors but he made it difficult to keep them. Without the help and encouragement of my brother and sister-in law I would have had a harder time. My husband had become like Jekyll and Hyde. He was very kind and loving at times and with little warning abusive and mean to me. He was critical of everything that I did. I was afraid to trust him and afraid not to.

By then I thought there must be something wrong with me since he could never be pleased. I thought that if I were better at everything then he would not act that way. I found a job and worked part-time. When I got home I picked up the children, cooked dinner, and did laundry. I would clean until one or two in the morning then get up at five to start a new day doing the same thing. It was never enough. It wasn't that he expected me to do all of that but

I thought it would make a difference in how he treated me if everything was nearly perfect.

After a few weeks I was hospitalized with total exhaustion. I really felt like a total failure then so I became more dependent on him. He seemed happier and easier to get along with when I was letting him have more control. Of course marriage shouldn't be about one controlling the other. It should be giving to each other. I was losing myself. I had always been independent but dependence on him seemed a small price to pay for peace and quiet.

Today I recognize this trait in so many women. It was years before I learned that abusive behavior follows this path. It is a control issue and makes the abuser feel more powerful giving them a sense of self -worth. It was also years before I felt free enough to admit that I was not responsible for his behavior. I did try to get him to see a counselor but he always said no that he did not have a problem. Satan was using his lack of self-worth and guilt over being neglected and abused as a child against him and me.

I saw no way out so I decided that I had to make the best of it. I had come to Atlanta with such high hopes but that seemed a lifetime ago. I decided that I had to get back to the reason for my being there. My true passion was writing and singing.

I could express my innermost thoughts when writing and had been keeping a journal for years. It started with my teenage diary where I would write my most private thoughts. I also wrote poems and songs beginning at age four-teen. Now my private journal became my self-proclaimed therapy. It was part of my healing.

The other part was seeking the God of my youth when it was convenient or needful. Otherwise I left Him on the shelf of my heart. I wrote many songs during that period of my life and toyed with the idea of picking up my dream of getting into music as a career. Music made me want to live again. I began to surround myself with writers and musicians. This was a major change in our lives. My husband was supportive to a point but it seemed every time I got close to success he pulled me back. He was never really comfortable with my having new people in my life but for a while allowed it.

I had met a wonderful lady that played piano and helped me to demo my songs. She had worked many years for a major local newspaper and had a plethora of friends. She introduced me to several interesting people in the arts and I made many new friends in music and writing circles. She believed in me and I so desperately needed someone to give me that nudge of encouragement. Mary accepted me and from her I learned to accept people for whom they are and appreciate their talents big or small. She helped me to dream again.

I want always to follow her example and encourage even the tiniest glimmer of hope in people I meet.

We never know what others are going through. Even Mary didn't know all the pressure that I was living under because I had gotten good at hiding it most of the time. At some point I began to be encouraged and went so far as to think I too could have it all. Earlier singer, Helen Reddy had released a song called "I am Woman". That was what I needed to hear. It was powerful.

I convinced my husband to drive me to auditions hours away where I would sing. I gave demos to artists and their agents hoping for a cut. Instead, I lost many songs that I had written. A few notes and words were changed and I was left with nothing. Some people in the business are totally unscrupulous. I was getting another taste of the real world and I didn't like the reality.

When I became pregnant with my second daughter I realized that time was slipping away. I had decided that I was going to record some of my own songs as soon as I could. After all Helen said that I could have it all.

Half -way through my pregnancy I was exposed to the measles. My OB/GYN gave me thousands of units of

Gamma Globulin but told me that there was a high chance that my baby would be deformed. He advised having an abortion with this child. It is still hard to think that people can just throw another living human being away because he or she may not be perfect. I would not even entertain the thought of killing my baby, I knew God would take care of her. Yes it was time to take Him off the shelf again.

The day finally came to welcome my new little girl to the family. I had hours of labor with no results so the doctor sent me home to walk. He told me to walk in the house all night if necessary to speed things up. By morning nothing had happened so I was admitted to the hospital. Her heartbeat was faint and the doctor forced the delivery with drugs. When my baby was born I kept waiting for them to bring her to me. No one ever would. Even my husband was making excuses for why it was taking so long.

Almost twenty four hours passed without seeing her so I went down the hall to find out for myself where she was. I was told that the nursery was full of newborns so several babies were in incubators in the hallway. I doubt that would happen today, thankfully.

I found her incubator and saw that she had a black bandage around her head to cover her eyes. She was so yellow I was frightened. At the time I did not know what jaundice looked like. Actually, I had never heard of it. The nurses finally explained what it was and I felt better. She weighed a little over six pounds at birth. She was under four pounds when I was released from the hospital. The hardest thing was leaving her there. God became real to me again during this trial. He was always there when I called and gave me comfort and assurance that all would be well with her. She came home when she weighed five pounds. She had no sucking instinct and we had to feed her around the clock for six weeks with a medicine dropper and a teaspoon. I could see that God was still in control of her life. Medical procedures have improved since then.

Soon after my check up my doctor resigned and took over one of the biggest abortion clinics in the state at that time. So many innocent children have lost their lives in the name of women's rights and greedy doctors. I thank God that my daughter was not one of them. How can a man or woman who has taken an oath to heal and preserve life be so heartless and commit such horrors on innocent babies. What a difference the lives of millions of murdered children would have made in America. I believe abortion is wrong and there is no justification. I do feel deep sadness for all the women young and old that have experienced the loss of a child through abortion. I pray that they will find healing.

By the time my daughter was six months old she was a happy, healthy child. I felt it was time to pursue my dream again.

I found a record producer in the city that we paid to demo my songs. He took all the Master copies of my songs to help me choose the right ones for recording. He made the arrangements and we went to a premier studio in Nashville to cut my first single record. It turned out great. In retrospect I realize that neither the A or B cut was a strong song. Still the record was sent to radio stations across the country and got lots of airplay. Response was good. The problem was that it was not distributed so there was no place to buy it.

I had about two hundred copies to sell at shows. Other than that the general public could not buy it.

A short time later the producer vanished with all my Master copies of new songs along with other writers' material. I never recovered my songs but some have surfaced through the years with a few changes. I did not have copyright on all of them. Lesson learned. I had believed the producer that told me that it wasn't necessary. Even now my naïve attitude about that situation astounds me.

About a year and a half later I got a call from the manager of a top recording artist. He asked if I could go to Miami to fill in for their female vocalist who had left to get married. I was so excited that I could hardly wait to tell my husband. The Star was a household name and I couldn't believe that they would choose me to sing with him. Some said that we could do anything and though I was not a libber I saw no reason that I couldn't take my family and enjoy this opportunity.

My husband was livid and would not hear of it. He said it was a career alone or my family but not both. To prove his point he took our two daughters and left. He was only gone for the day but it sent me into a sinking depression. Of course I was not going to have a career without my children so once again I gave in. There was never any compromise. This time I couldn't shake it off. My life seemed hopeless. Surely marriage was not supposed to be this way. Couldn't God see how bad things were in our life? Why didn't He fix it? After a while I quit trying. For months I struggled to get through the daily routine of life. Finally the doctor gave me a little pill called Valium. It helped enough to mask the pain. Trying to keep busy I managed to find a part-time job though I had no interest in it.

STATE OF GRACE

I had a teenage girl come to my house to baby sit for a few hours a day that summer. She lived close by and my children loved having her with them.

While my little girls were playing in the front yard two men drove up and tried to get them into the car. Their screams and quick thinking by the sitter prevented a double tragedy. Though I had turned my back on God I could still see His Grace and protection for my children and thankfulness flooded my soul. A few weeks later my oldest daughter was playing out back. She was about four at the time.

I was in the kitchen looking out the window when I saw her run to the side street. We had always taught them never to go to strangers. By the time I got to her a clean-cut, grandfatherly man was holding her in his arms about to put her in his car. She was smiling and didn't appear to be afraid at all.

I never knew how he managed to convince her to go to him and why she would be so trusting. All of our warnings had been futile. I learned that we could never take for granted how our children would respond and that they must be close at all times to be protected.

I ran out the door yelling and flew across the yard to get her. The motor was running and the door was open. He obviously panicked when I arrived and threw her into my arms instead of the car. He never said a word. He sped away and was not found. About a week later a child was found murdered in the woods across the street. God had spared my daughter for a second time.

I was grateful but coping one day at a time. My marriage was worse than ever. When I awoke I took Valium. When I went to sleep I took Valium. The "valley of the dolls" were taking their toll on me. Soon I stayed in my bathrobe night and day. I was too depressed to get dressed so I rarely left the house. I had little patience with the children and I just wanted to sleep through my husbands' attitude and anger. When I was awake enough I started binge eating and my weight ballooned to a whopping one-hundred and forty two pounds. My neighborhood acquaintances insisted that I should diet with them. I had only one friend in the bunch. My children played with their children so that was the tie between us. My two other friends were not in that crowd. They all could hardly believe that I had gained so much weight from my usual one-hundred and twenty-five pounds when they met me. I had gained seven-teen pounds. At five foot and seven inches I wasn't that big but I began to believe that I was hideously fat. With their help and shakes that they made after every walk I exercised and dieted my way up to one-hundred and sixty pounds. They seemed satisfied then and left me alone. What are friends for? Right?

Food became my replacement for affection, fun and any other emotional needs that I had. When that didn't work I had the little white dolls as my escape. My escapes were becoming my biggest trap. There were many changes taking place with the only three women I could truly call friends.

One was from England and her husband was in the military. They were being transferred soon and I was dreading the day when we would have to say goodbye. It wasn't the move that forced the goodbye though. She developed breast cancer and died within a very short time. Another friend had cancer in her leg. She had the same type tumors that I had previously. The doctor removed part of her leg and a few months later her entire hip. I felt helpless to do any more than make her family meals or care for her children occasionally. That was a struggle when I could barely care for mine. It was God's loving grace and protection that kept us all safe as I drove them to and from school often driving still wearing my housecoat.

She never knew how bad things were of course. She didn't need my burdens. Deb died an agonizing death. My other friend was dying from a muscle disease. My sweet Mary that had helped me so much was suffering in silence. She never complained. In two years they were all gone. Instead of calling on God during this time I was thinking, what was the use. I was not just feeling sorry for myself but we were still living in a nightmare marriage and I felt little hope. I have since learned we have to choose hope and love and all the positive things in our lives. We cannot rely only on our feelings. If we do we will be swallowed up by life.

A woman in the neighborhood usually went walking every Saturday and always seemed to stop by at the most inopportune time. I didn't know her well and didn't want to really. Before leaving she would invite me to her Church. I could see the church from my yard but had never attended. It was a "Pentecostal" and I was a "Baptist", of course. I want to say LOL! I can almost hear God laughing at our labels and separation. Yes I do believe that God has a sense of humor.

This lady had a glow I had never seen before and always seemed so happy. She told me that she was a single Mom with five children and a full time job. She lived in a small apartment and had no car and very little of anything else yet she always seemed to be smiling. She would always want to pray when she came by or tell me that she was praying for me when she left. I wondered how she could be so happy and cheerful. I wanted no part of getting to know her. After all, how could she possibly understand what I was going through. God was sending help my way through a precious, Godly woman but I couldn't see it then. I had experienced two more miscarriages and lost three friends in two years. Death was all around me. I didn't want to feel anything anymore and Valium helped to make that possible.

It was between doses of little, white pills that was so hard for me to cope so I took more and more. It is easy to become addicted. Once we give over to the power of drugs, prescription or illegal then we are captive. All I had to do was call the pharmacy and they would call my doctor and get a refill on my prescription anytime I wanted it. I didn't even have to get out of the car. I could go through the drive-thru window. I didn't even have to dress and went many times in my bathrobe. Valium was the drug of choice in my Atlanta suburb and it flowed freely.

There was an especially horrible fight with my husband the night before and I just wanted the pain to stop. I was in the deepest depression that I had ever known. I had no thought or desire to kill myself. I was in the kitchen and had poured the Valium into my hand and was taking one at a time between periods of sobbing. The hurt and sheer abandonment that I felt was so overwhelming. Somehow it had to end. A few more dolls and I would feel better I thought.

The girls were in the next room playing. My youngest daughter came into the room and asked, "What are you doing Mommy"? I could vaguely hear her as if from a distance. I could not respond because it felt like a dream. She left and came back two more times asking the same question. By then I was on the floor leaning against a cabinet.

She shook my shoulder over and over. She got me awake enough that I realized what I was doing and was able to make myself throw up. On that kitchen floor I promised God that if He would let me live to raise my children I would surrender it all. I had come to the end of myself and who was beside me still but Almighty God. His mercy was real. He had never left me. He was waiting for me to come back to Him.

I would like to say that I was instantly freed from the desire of drugs but my body still craved them and it was a hard process to walk it out. The doctor actually gave me another drug to take its place and ease me off. Gods' grace was sufficient during that trial as well.

The child that my doctor had wanted to kill in abortion God had used to save my life. My youth, energy and ambition were all focused on temporal goals.

The pain of my life was so deep that I wasn't objective, allowing a husband to dictate my worth. His pain was so deep he acted the only way that he knew how. Through it all I lost sight of my first love.

NIV (Jeremiah 24:7) "Then I will give them a heart to know me, that I am the Lord; and they shall be My people and I will be their God, for they shall return to me with their whole heart."

FAITH: WALK IT OUT

Once again my neighbor and new friend came to visit. This time when she invited me to go to church I could hardly wait to go. I had decided months earlier that I would go just so that she would leave me alone. I never had but this time my motives were right. The love of God had shown through her for so long, witnessing, reminding, wooing me to Him. I was excited for the first time in a long time.

The next day I rededicated my life to God and purposed in my heart to live as good a life as I could. There was still much for me to learn though. Decisions and determination are never enough. It takes surrender in every area of life, letting God live through us. It took many years for me to learn this truth and still I fail. It sounds so simple but life's lessons are never learned in one day or one season. It is naive to think that we are in the driver's seat. We don't just live life we experience it. Every action causes reaction and responsibility. It is all about choices. Intellectually I reasoned that I should have a happy "normal" life now. Sanctification is a real process of shaking and changing us, usually one step at a time. God allows things in our lives to bring us to submission and tries to remove the impurities to make us more like Christ.

NIV (Luke 22:31) "And the Lord said, "Simon, Simon, Satan has asked to sift all of you as wheat." (Luke 22:32) "But I have prayed for you Simon that your faith may not fail and when you have turned back strengthen your brother.

Satan had to get permission from God to try Peter, just as I was being tried. It is a refining process that makes us more pliable in God's hands. He is the Potter. We are the clay. We can't be used if we refuse to be molded in the image of Christ. Totally self-sufficient people do not see a need for God. We are weak and inadequate without Him. If we are rooted and grounded in His Presence then we will understand the "sifting" process and be stronger for it. Gold is sifted through a sieve to separate the gold from the sand. Treasure is usually hidden. God wants to find the jewel in everyone that he knows is hidden in our human condition so we are tried through many different ways. If we rebel and blame God or someone else then the process may go on longer.

Every day we are faced with decisions. Often we make choices with no thought to the consequences. If we consider a decision to be important we give it more time and consideration. There are many examples in scripture of decisions changing circumstances in mighty ways. The deciding factor is always whether God is put into the equation. Do we pray and seek Gods counsel? Look at the example of Daniel. (Daniel 1:8) He was a captive in Babylon. In his heart he chose not to defile himself with the king's meat or with the wine which he drank. As a result of making the right choice he had Gods favor. He and his companions had a miraculous intervention in the lion's den and the fiery furnace.

Our refining may include physical suffering. That is not always the case. Sickness comes because we have made bad decisions such as overeating, eating unhealthy foods, smoking, and so many other life altering choices. There are many unhealthy habits that are detrimental to our bodies. We can have a stubborn, unrelenting will that affects our health and well-being through stress. However, sometimes sickness puts us on our knees then God can get our undivided attention. Often we are content to live as we have been doing because it is too much effort to change things.

If we depend on money or ourselves instead of God then finances can be taken away. We are to honor God with our finances. After all it is His to begin with.

(MALACHI 3: 10 "Bring the whole tithe into the storehouse that there may be food in my house, Test me in this," says the Lord Almighty" and see if I will not open the floodgates of heaven and pour out so much blessing that there will not be room enough to store."

I sincerely believe that we are to give the first ten per cent back to God. The first fruits are His to bless others and do the work of ministry. I believe we are blessed by what we give over that. Those two ways are essential to me and I believe in giving to the ministry that feeds my spirit. God will direct us in our giving if we ask. I enjoy looking for ways to give and pray that God will always give me the desire to give as if I am giving directly to Him.

We don't give to get but to be able to bless others and for the joy of giving. Aside from tithes and offerings it doesn't always have to be money that we give. Giving time, food, clothing or a day of babysitting to a new mother can mean so much to them. If we believe in sowing and reaping then I think we would all agree if we plant (sow) money then we will reap money. If we sow beans in a garden we will reap beans. It is the same principle. No matter how much or how little we had when I was growing up my wise Mother always said to give the best that we had not what was left over. After all, it was to be given as if we were giving directly to Jesus the King.

We are tried through different measures but we must remember that God is in control. If we are saved He will not let us endure more than we can handle. We will be tested until we can be used. Sometimes we can get in a spiritual rut and are content to live as we always have since getting saved. We can also take for granted Gods mercy and grace. God can and often does get our attention and stretch our faith by letting us go through trials.

NEW GROUND

Once I began attending the Pentecostal Church where my new friend went I learned truth and true worship. They taught directly from the Bible. Holy Spirit was an integral part of that teaching and He manifest His Presence in many ways that I was unfamiliar with.

There was no legalism there. God in all His Identity was real and His principles were applicable in my everyday life. My faith grew by leaps and bounds.

My two little girls were growing physically and spiritually and they were learning more about Jesus. They learned bible verses and songs and their curiosity seemed endless. My older daughter had begun to question me and asked all kinds of things about Jesus. One day as I was writing songs and recording demos they were both wanting to help. My youngest little girl wanted to sing in the mic and her sister wanted to write and record a song. Trying to appease them I thought that it would be a good project to let them record a song.

From her questions I wrote this song.

MAMA WILL YOU TELL ME ABOUT JESUS

Mama Will You Tell Me About Jesus
The Little Boy That Was Born With That Name
Mama Will You Tell Me All About Jesus
The Way He Lived And Died On The Cross In Pain.

Will You Tell Me All About How Jesus Loves Me,
How He Watches Us And Keeps Us In His Care
Will You Tell Me How He Made Me For You And Daddy
And How When I Pray I Know He's Always There

Now Mama Will You Talk With Me To Jesus
Let's Tell Him How We All Love Him Today
And Mommy, Don't Forget To Ask Sweet Jesus
If He Will Teach My Daddy How To Pray

© 2015 Glenda Vaughn
© 2015 OUR DESTINY MUSIC PUBLISHING BMI

My children showed a measure of faith that really surprised me that day. I was so thankful for the teaching of our new church and how happy they were while attending there.

I was glad that we had shared those few moments and the loving innocence of small children to see the real picture. They loved their daddy and they realized that he needed Jesus.

Glenda Vaughn

NIV (Hebrews11:1) Now FAITH is confidence in what we hope for and assurance about what we do not see."

I believed that anything was possible! Faith is believing that God will do as He said.

It is simply, trusting Him to honor His word. Our responsibility is to rest in Him going about our daily lives knowing that He is in control.

Through the fellowship of the church I felt strengthened and began to pray for my husbands' salvation. I knew that God would reach him if he would just open his heart. I was committed to him and was sure we would eventually be happy. Once again our marriage was on steadier ground and I truly believed that everything would be alright with us. We decided to have one more child. I really felt that we were supposed to have a son. A son was going to complete our family so we were ecstatic when he was on the way.

A gentle, loving husband emerged again. We prepared the layette, chose his name and waited.

I ignored the warning when he wasn't growing like he should have been. I had believed for a son and would not accept that God would let anything go wrong. I reached the fifth month of pregnancy when I noticed that there was very little movement. I had stopped gaining weight as well. By the sixth month there was no heartbeat either.

After tests the doctor told me that I had cancer cells and that was probably what had killed our son. They were not sure at that point. The doctors said I would never have another child because I had to have a hysterectomy. We were heartbroken and couldn't believe that this would happen? The emptiness was overwhelming. I had been counting down the weeks when I could hold my little boy.

KJV (Matthew 6:6) "But you, when you pray, go into your room and when you have shut the door, pray to your Father who is in the secret place; and your Father, who sees in secret will reward you openly."

Late in the night, before the scheduled surgery I called my Pastor who agreed with me that God was going to work it out. I went into surgery in peace fully trusting my Father to take over. The doctor took the son my heart was aching for. I didn't know what God would do but I knew He would do something and everything would be as He planned.

When I awakened from surgery the doctor seemed stunned!

He said there was no cancer and he did not do a hysterectomy. He said he couldn't explain it but there was scar tissue as if surgery had already been done. God was the Physician that day! All the tears we shed wouldn't bring back our son. The heartache wouldn't change what happened but the results reminded me that God would keep his promise! We would have a son.

Glenda Vaughn

Though I knew that God would be faithful, when I got home it was so much effort to put my baby's things away. Hopes and dreams for this boy were gone and tears flowed as I packed up his belongings along with my favorite outfit, his tiny baseball suit. I mourned the loss of Daniel Patrick and my empty arms ached to hold him. All I could do was hold his clothes and wish he were there.

I wasn't sure when we would have another baby but within three months we were expecting another child. I had no doubt that it was a boy and proceeded to pick out a name. I asked Gods help in choosing the right name for this boy. Into the fourth month the pregnancy became difficult. I was having premature contractions so the doctor told me to drink a glass of wine every day to relax and be able to carry this child.

By the eight month the amniotic fluid leaked out and I was hospitalized. The fluid was checked and it was determined that my baby's lungs and kidneys were not developed enough to sustain him. He was given a shot in vitro to develop them faster. The doctor said that the chance of the sac refilling with fluid and sealing was very slim but that he would wait for a few hours before taking him. He said it would be a miracle if it did and that the chances were few. I said but God can do anything.

Many people in my family and my church prayed believing. Within a few hours the sac was refilled and sealed. Again

46

the doctors were amazed! God is Wonderful! Only He could have done that. It was out of human hands.

NIV (Psalm 4:5) 'Many, Lord my God, are the wonders You have done, the things You have planned for us. None can compare with You: were I to speak and tell of Your deeds they would be too many to declare."

A month later our son was born. He came into the world weighing almost ten pounds with a head full of dark hair and beautiful blue eyes.

He was such a beautiful boy but to our horror he had a tumor on his head. His doctors said it was an encephala hematoma and that he would be crippled, brain damaged and probably blind. There was too much pressure on his brain. With that news we were sent home.

I knew that we had a special son because Satan was trying so hard to destroy him. It was devastating news. Why would God allow such a thing? I didn't understand but somehow I knew that God had a plan. We took him home and the Pastor and Elders from my "new church" came and anointed him with oil and prayed over him. Nathan which means "our gift from God," was healed that afternoon.

We all watched as the tumor shrank a little at a time and in about four hours it had disappeared. Once again God was God, the healer. Jehovah-Rapha was in the house.

(Psalm 103: 1) "Praise the Lord, o my soul; all my inmost being Praise His Holy Name (Psalm 103: 3) who forgives all your sins and heals all your diseases."

We took Nathan to a specialist who confirmed what we already knew. God had healed our son. However, the doctor was not willing to say that God had healed him. He said there must have been a mistake on the diagnosis. We knew better. We saw it and had the other doctor reports and tests. His unbelief or pride or whatever it was would not make us doubt what we knew and what we had seen with our own eyes. Some call it Providence. I call it Faithfulness by our Almighty God.

Many people are taught that healing is not for today. God is the same healer today as He was when the woman with the issue of blood touched the hem of his garment and was made well. He will be the same God, whatever we need. God is the same yesterday, today and forevermore. Some of our churches have limited what God is allowed to do. Our mistaken teachings have hindered our faith. Scripture is full of examples of healings and there are lessons to be learned by their examples.

NIV (John 9:1) 'As he went along he saw a man blind from birth, His disciples asked Him, "Rabbi who sinned, the man or his parents, that he was made blind?" "Neither the man or his parents sinned, said Jesus, but this happened so that the works of God might be displayed in him. As long as it is day we must do the works of him who sent me. Night is coming, when no one can work. While I am in the world I am the light of the world."

We must not pick and choose what to believe from the Bible based on others opinions. We have to trust and believe what God says in His Word. Seek Him in Spirit and truth and realize that you can have what God says that you can have. Take Him at His Word. Choose life. Enjoy your salvation and all the blessings that come with it. Trust Him to be concerned with whatever concerns you. He loves you!

When Nathan was a few weeks old I took him to church and dedicated him to the Lord. God had kept his promise to me. I promised God that I would teach my son about Him. I did sincerely try to teach all of my children about the Lord. Could I have done more? Of course I could. I'm sure that I missed many opportunities but I am assured that they have heard the Word and know the voice of God. I treasure the prayer times we shared while they were growing up. It is now their responsibility to accept His direction for their lives by surrendering their will to Him. Teaching our children about spiritual matters is a heavy responsibility for parents and many take it too lightly.

In the scriptures there are many instructions on how to raise our children. Yes, there is an instruction book. Many times new parents have said, why don't babies come with a manual? In actuality, they do. It is called the Bible.

Many new parents seek out information from doctors and authors some of which have never had a child. It is never too early to proclaim Gods' Word to your children and it's never too late to start. Build a foundation. I heard something very powerful when my children were young. Someone said, talk about your children to God more than you talk about God to your children. Speak the Word to them and speak The Word over them. That is the way to bless your children. His Word is alive and powerful.

NIV (Isaiah 55:11) so is My Word that goes out from my mouth: It will accomplish what I desire and achieve the purpose for which I send it. The Bible has it all plus help from Holy Spirit if we rely on Him.

NIV (Deuteronomy 6:5-7 Love the Lord your God with all your heart and with all your soul and with all your strength. (6) These commandments that I give you today are to be on your hearts. (7) Impress them on your children. Talk about them when you sit at home and when you walk along the road, when you lie down and when you get up.

These are not just suggestions. It is our responsibility to teach them. We can use all the help we can get. That is one reason I am so thankful for the teaching children receive in Sunday school and in vacation bible school where they are taught to remember scripture, hiding Gods Word in their heart.

It will be brought to mind years after they are grown when it is needed. God's word is living and it will accomplish what it is sent to do according to scripture.

NIV (Proverbs 22:6) "Train up a child in the way he should go and when he is old he will not turn from it." I believe that this means that we teach them ourselves and not leave it up to the church to do it.

(2 Timothy 3:15-16) and how from infancy you have known the Holy Spirit which is able to make you wise for salvation through faith in Christ Jesus. (16) All scripture is God breathed and is useful for teaching, rebuking, correcting and training in righteousness.

All of my children have had challenges but I look forward to the day when each of them realize their true talents and calling. I pray that each one of my children, grandchildren and great grandchildren will be obedient to what God calls them to do with their lives. They will have to listen with their heart.

Hopefully they will not procrastinate and have a stubborn will like their parents have had. I know that they will be faith filled, praying Christians. I trust that they will commit to Christ Jesus everything that they do and live in His safety and the peace that comes from surrendering to His will. Each one has a special gift and I want them to devote it to God who gave it to them. I believe in speaking to our children what God says about them. As a nation I believe we have failed to bless our children with positive words that God has given for exhortation. We are seeing so many in this generation of youth that have little self –esteem. They need to know their worth and be told who God says that they are.

Once they are taught if they are wise they will seek Gods' wisdom in every situation and decision that they are faced with. I want them all to know Joy that comes from serving others for Christ. I am blessed to know that my children do think of others and have shown in real deeds how they are concerned for ones less fortunate. They all have empathy for the homeless especially and do help in many ways. They give food, clothing and money. We have worked side by side in the mission kitchen preparing food for the people from the streets. My youngest daughter has even taken a few people into her home on occasion. I want them to please God and not want for the worlds' approval. After all, the world can give us nothing that will matter through eternity. The only thing we take to heaven is our love and deeds while we were here.

I know that Holy Spirit will lead my adult children and their families into righteousness. I want them to have a tender heart that is open to His word so that His words will take root. I never want their hearts to be hardened and my prayer often is that God will tender their hearts when life stresses get them down. If they will follow His leading He will take them in the right direction.

Following Him will save them so much heartache. The world has so many stresses and attractions it is a battle for even mature Christians so if we keep our minds on Christ Jesus we all will find strength in coping with life struggles. Our prayer should always be that all of our children will have a passion for Jesus and love Him with all their heart, soul, strength and mind.

I don't want my children to fall as I have through all these years. I pray that they will be stronger and not falter. More than anything I want them to be sure of their salvation and know that we will be together with Christ for eternity. That is a serious decision that all must make. Parents should never leave the responsibility of making sure of their children's salvation to someone else when a child's eternal life is at stake.

When we let down our guard and don't spend time with the Lord we are faced with temptations and lack of commitment. This will cause our flesh to make decisions that we will not make if our minds are stayed on Him.

NIV (Ephesians 10:12) "For our struggle is not against flesh and blood but against the rulers, against the authorities, against the powers of this dark world and against the spiritual forces of evil in the heavenly realms."

NIV (Philippians 4:8) 'Finally brothers and sisters, whatever is true, whatever is noble, whatever is right, whatever is lovely, whatever is admirable, if anything is excellent or praiseworthy, think on these things."

The son that the doctors predicted would lie crippled and brain damaged has never had a serious illness. He graduated from a major University and is successful in a business career. I know that God has a special purpose for his life. He has not yet realized that he has a gift for teaching but it is clear to me and I am anxious to have him honor God with his gifts and talents.

God honored my prayers and prayers of others on our behalf. He honored our faith in Him and did for our son and my family what only God could do. He has intervened in the lives of all my children at many intervals in their lives. Each one has special talents and gifts that I am anxious for them to discover and use for God's service. I am so blessed to be their Mother.

He is Jehovah-Elohim- The Mighty One ! He is Covenant keeping Creator. We know that to be true. In Hebrew Lord is equivalent to Jehovah. God equals Elohim.

I am including the many names of God and what they mean. God is God and there is no other. To know Him through the many attributes that His Names possess gives me a better understanding of the depth of His love.

1. Jehovah-Lord-(Isaiah 26:4)
2. Elohim-The Mighty One-(Genesis 1:1)
3. Jehovah Elohim-Covenant Keeping Creator-(Genesis 2:4)
4. El Elyon- The Most High God-Genesis 14:18)
5. Adonai- The Sovereign Master-(Genesis 15:1-2)
6. El Shaddai-The Sufficient God-(Genesis 17:1)
7. Jehovah Jireh-The Lord will Provide-(Genesis 22:14)
8. Jehovah-Rapha-The Lord that Heals-(Exodus 15:26)
9. Jehovah-Nissi- The Lord My Banner-(Exodus 17:15)
10. Jehovah-McKaddesh-The Lord Who Sanctifies-(Leviticus 20:5)
11. Jehovah –Sabbath-The Lord of Hosts-(1 Samuel 1:3)
12. Jehovah-Shalom-The Lord Our Peace-(Judges 6:24)
13. Jehovah-Roi-The Lord My Shepherd-(Psalms 23:1)
14. Jehovah Tsidkenu-The Lord Our Righteousness-(Jeremiah 23:6)
15. Jehovah Shammah-(The Lord Is There- (Ezekiel 48:35)

PRAYER-OUR LIFELINE

Prayer is an integral part of our being if we are to be close to the Father and be His effective servants. We are so privileged to be able to go to Him through Jesus. Prayer is not the means to an end but the communion of our spirits with God. He speaks to us through scripture, other people and impressions that we may get while in prayer.

Building a relationship with the Father leads to a life of holiness as we lay down our worldly ways. True prayer won't change Gods' purpose but is an effort to release our cares to the one who is in control. If we are sincerely seeking His guidance then we will accept His answers and put aside concern for the situation. Listen to what God says to you. He wants us to know His will in every area of our lives. Talking to someone that we love should be simple. Praying to God is just telling Him what is on our mind. It is easy and we don't have to use flowery words or expressions to get His attention. He already knows us anyway so honesty and sincerity is all that He wants. To me prayer is as necessary as food and water to sustain my life and rest in His guidance.

Our character is strengthened while we are spending time in His Presence as well as overcoming life struggles. It is built through having a desire to be more like Christ. We should start each new day in prayer committing it to God. We always need His help and guidance. More credence is given to our prayers when we know beyond a doubt that God is listening and ready to do what we ask in His will. We can then be confident that He will act on our behalf. He will always give His wisdom if we ask and listen. We must focus on our relationship with God which we do in prayer, praise and worship.

NIV (Psalm 145:) "I will exalt You, my God, the King. I will Praise Your Name for ever and ever. Every day I will Praise You."

NIV (John 4: 24) God is spirit and His worshippers must worship in the Spirit and in truth)

A life of prayer leads us down the road to holiness. The road is paved with hard lessons on the way to Sanctification. To be made more like Jesus can be harder for some than others. We have to lay it all on the altar. We have to surrender anxiety, rejection, anger, fear, loneliness and uncertainty about our future. We have to get all the negative things out of our heart to be able to have room for all the plans and purpose that God has for us!

NIV (Jeremiah 1: 4-5) "Before I formed you in the womb I knew you, before you were born I set you apart; I appointed you as a prophet to the nations."

I have a favorite saying by an unknown person. It says, If I could live my life over I would find You sooner so I could love you longer. This is what I think of when I think of Jesus.

He is my closest companion through Holy Spirit. If we allow Holy Spirit to speak through us then we are praying in the spirit, our prayer language. This spiritual connection has been so confusing to so many because of doctrinal differences in many churches. It is clearly scriptural. People miss a deeper relationship because of not going far enough in prayer. This deeper realm is not for a select few but for any Christian wanting a deeper spiritual walk. Some refer to this praying as "speaking in tongues". This is our secret place and Satan cannot enter or interfere with our prayers. This is true communion with Father God and should be our highest goal. In scripture we are commanded to pray.

KJV (Philippians 4:6) says, "Be careful for nothing but in everything by prayer and supplication with thanksgiving let your requests be made known unto God."

KJV Philippians (4:7) And the peace of God, which passeth all understanding, shall keep your hearts and minds through Christ Jesus."

It is speaking, waiting and listening for Him to speak. Not always, but many times when I need a specific word about a situation I keep a notebook with me. I listen after I pray. I write down what I hear in my spirit that Father is saying to me. You can recognize God's voice by what He says about Himself. Be aware that Satan counterfeits. He does not glorify God or Jesus. Satan can't interfere when you pray in the spirit but he may try to make you doubt your answer if you let him. The content of what God says about Himself and how He guides is another way to know it is truly God speaking. Often He will bring scripture to mind.

KJV (John 10:27) "My sheep hear My voice and I know them and they follow Me".)

As an example I am including a few pages that I've written, through the years as God spoke to me. Often I could not write as fast as He spoke. I call them my love letters and though they are very personal to me, I want you to understand what I'm talking about. I usually have to go back and read them after I'm through writing because I don't always comprehend everything as I write. Some are dated some are not. These span many years but I'm including only a few. I have many more and the words that He has said to me have been a comfort and guidance to me in many situations.

LOVE LETTERS

October 2, 1991 – I have given you hurts from My Hand to grow you into my likeness. I superseded events in your life to protect you from Satan's evil will against you. I am your heavenly Father who watches over all. I see My cup (you) half full of the oil of My Spirit but it will overflow like running water and healing will come to many. Their scars are deep and only My oil will heal the wounds that Satan has inflicted. They will come. Pray with them and for them. Their spirits are sweet but unnatural in My Goodness. Speak to them of My Love to all who will receive. I am ever present in your life and theirs, even when they are unaware. I am your Father. You are My child. My love abounds to you.

#2 My purpose for you is undeniable. My plans exceed your plans. No I do not think you foolish. You are My child after My own heart. You have just taken too many turns, go straight. Trust Me and not your own devices. I will lead if you will follow me. You are the sheep I am the shepherd. Listen to My voice and heed it only. Every decision must pass by and before Me. Lay them at My feet. I will abide and guide. Take time with Me. You are My child. Yes you must go when I say. Trust me El Paso is on My agenda. New York I will work out. Trust Me, you can do much good.

(I have been to New York and had a special experience there. I am waiting to go and see what He brings about in El Paso.)

#3 In peace, I am with you always even to the ends of the earth. Wherever you may travel wherever you may roam take Me along. I will be at your side. Get to know me as you once did. Spend time in My Presence. I will greet you and make you comfortable because I am your resting place. I am your shield. I will guard you from the stress of life. Know My Joy, surrender all. You will be light when you have no burdens to carry for I carried them all for you on the Cross. They did not take My life. I gave it for you freely. I am Lord.

#4 I will protect and save you and a willow shall be cast forth before Me and your eyes will behold a vessel filled to overflowing. Yes, a child I will fill to overflowing with My Holy Spirit and he will speak to all the land for I called him at a young age and he will bend to My Heart and ways as a willow bends with the wind and I will blow upon him and anoint him to speak My Word, to speak of

Me for I am to be praised. He will lift Me up. I AM GOD, JEHOVAH-JIREH.

#5 May 1995- I speak as a Father knowing my child has eyes and ears for Me listening to your cries and knowing you will return to Me. I am stable and I give light to your path. I will teach you step by step. By day I will lead you. That is why you must always look up and know that I am God, Alpha-Omega. Trust in My sight for I see further down the road of your life than you can comprehend. I know what is safe distance and you must let Me lead. Don't try to travel ahead of Me. Look to Me, your God, your Father.

#6 July 13, 1998 I have not forsaken you daughter nor will I ever. I hold you in the Palm of My hand. My tender mercies extend to you all the day long. I will grant to you what you ask for I know you ask with a tender heart for Me. I am your Father. Ask what you will. I will not blind you. Accept Me for who I am, Living God. Yes I said Living God. You do not worship a stone that cannot produce life for I am a Life-Giver. I will protect and enable you for I am Father God. You are my child and life blood will be carried to others through and by you. You are My disciple and I am well pleased. Do not fret about failing. You are human and I do understand. Stand with Me daily. Walk with Me daily. I will keep you ever more, I am your God. Do not leave Me. I am strict with you because I expect much. I have taught you many years. Now it is time to teach and tell others of My Great Love and My Promises. I will not withhold good from you. I am your Father. You can trust me. You have trusted others and they have let you down. They do not know Me. They do not accept or even see My Love but you, daughter know Me. Walk with Me and I will teach you still. You are concerned for others as I am. I am concerned for you. Do not forget it. My concern over rides all your problems and you must leave them with Me. I will not disappoint you as others have. I am your God. I am your Maker. I know you well. I see potential in all you do for Me even when you think you have failed. Arise My daughter, you are My child and I will walk with you on lonely days and nights. You can call on Me for I will be here for you always. Come talk with me again. Yes, tomorrow and all tomorrows for I look for you to spend time with Me. I understand you and my heart spills over with love for you. Yes, you can trust Me for you love Me too and I will never let you down. Stay close daughter, My Love surrounds you. I will let you know more of Me. If you even ask I will do it. Your God.

#7 I am your Father. My path is clear. Walk steadfastly on My road to wisdom, understanding and knowledge for I am waiting to welcome you with a rod of hope for I am the Good Shepherd. You are my servant. Don't worry. Nathan is in my keeping. Growing up is hard but I will not take My Eyes off Nathan, Ryan, Christy or Kim.

Glenda Vaughn

You must always be an obedient soldier in my army to save the lost souls of this world. I am your buckler. I am your righteousness. I am your keeper. Lean on Me for all righteousness not to your understanding. Jobs are many, plentiful. I will lead to the right one. Do not fear. It is not a problem. I will bless as many waters rush over your soul and ripples shall engulf you. Seek My Face. Listen to My Voice of love. Serve Me in song, music! (but I am not a good singer, Lord.) "but I Am, Praises will Exalt Me,"

#8 Glen you are my shining vessel. You are one of the broken vessels that I have healed and am filling with My Word and My Presence. I love spending time with you. I know that you are sincere in wanting to please Me. I am pleased. I will lift you up and I will give blessings because you are faithful daughter in trying to please me. Yes it has been hard for you but I will fill your lonely days for I made you. I know how you think and what you need You need My love most of all daughter and I will send it to you in many ways because you want to please Me, your Father and I want to please you, My child, My daughter.

#9 The daughter that I'm looking for is but a heartbeat away from My heart and is filled with My love. You are My daughter child and I know you will serve Me with a servants' heart but I love you like a Papa loving his own. You are a widow in a lonely land in many ways but I am your Father and your Husband. I am everything and all you need. I am God.

I realize that not all who read these "letters" will agree with my familiarity with Almighty God and may look upon them as less than reverent. He is my Father and the bond we share will never be broken. It is real and precious to me.

NIV (Isaiah 30:21) Whether you turn to the right or to the left your ears will hear a voice behind you saying, This is the way; walk in it.

Prayer is an essential part of having a relationship with God. It is timeless and we are all reaping the benefits of prayers that were prayed in generations past. Our parents and grandparents called on God for their families many years before we were ever born. God has not forgotten and is still answering those cries on our behalf. We know the value and blessing of having someone pray for us. So many times I have heard someone say, "I would not be here if it were not for my praying mother or grandmother." There have been songs written that say the same thing.

Our intercession for our families will go on as well. Prayer opens the door for God to bring about healing, deliverance, restoration and miracles. Our interceding for others will bring results if we pray in faith in the name of Jesus. I ask God to open their hearts to receive and know Him. I ask Him to open their ears to know His voice above the sounds of the world and the voice of Satan.

I have a niece that I had talked to about salvation but she still had many questions and comparisons. I didn't know what else to do so I felt that I should pray for her spiritual ears to be opened. Early one morning I received a phone call from her. She said that she had dreamed that someone was pulling cotton from out of her ears. When she woke it was clear what we had talked and prayed about. She was hearing with her spiritual ears. She then asked Jesus into her heart. Just as I often do, I prayed His Word. I prayed His promises back to Him because I knew that it would bring results. It is not a magical formula. Scripture says that God's Word will not return to Him void. It is also important to plead the blood over the ones you are interceding for. Satan is always ready to try to steal their souls.

NIV (1 John 4:4) "You dear children, are from God and have overcome them, because the one who is in you is greater than the one who is in the world".

David prayed in the Psalms that God would accept his prayer. He was a man after Gods' own heart. He sinned, committing adultery but God forgave him. David loved God and he was a true worshiper. We all exist to worship God and when we worship in sincerity and obedience we will want to be no more than a servant to do what

He wills because we love Him. When our attitude is that of a servant it brings humility and then God can use us. Father will then lead us to our destiny. We all have a divine purpose.

Another story in the Bible reminds me that Gods plan is to bring about our destiny even when we are not aware that what is happening in our lives is to fulfill God's purpose. I have always loved the story of Joseph and his brothers that sold him into slavery. They deceived their father Jacob into thinking that Joseph was dead because they were jealous of him.

They said that he was a dreamer and they sold him to Egyptians for twenty pieces of silver. I remember this story from childhood because of his coat of many colors. God put Joseph where he needed to be. Joseph was a natural leader and when he was made a governor in Egypt he was in a position to help many people and keep them from starving. I like the story because he was re-united with his father and was able to forgive his brothers and show Gods love to them through compassion and mercy. What was meant for evil God used for their blessing. That is a good lesson for us all.

NIV (Psalms 141: "May my prayer be set before you like incense; may the lifting up of my hands be like the evening sacrifice."

Prayer sustains us and we gain strength relying on the Lord. We need to listen with our heart and from the depths of our spirit dwell with Him. There is so much that I want to relate about prayer. Most of you probably know what I am sharing but it is important and bears repeating. God puts the desire in us to want to pray. If we are obedient and listening then we know when Holy Spirit is directing us. God has directed me and answered more prayers for me than I can even remember.

One of the latest ones that has impacted my life has to do with my music co-writer and singing partner. We have become best friends over the last couple of years and both recognize that our meeting was directed by God. I was getting several invitations to attend different songwriter rounds in Nashville, Tennessee and had not attended any of them. My sons encouraged me to go and one of them, the other songwriter in the family agreed to accompany me. After the first meeting I felt that this would be a wonderful group to be associated with and returned for another gathering the following week. Before going that time I had been in deep prayer about a move that I felt strongly about. I had the feeling that I was supposed to move to the mountains. I didn't know anyone in the mountains nor did I know which mountain. Knowing there was music in Gatlinburg, Tennessee I assumed that would be the place. However, I kept hearing a name in my spirit that I had never heard before. Finally I said, Lord I trust You to show me where I am supposed to go and know that You must make a way.

I took out a State map and closed my eyes and asked God where. I pointed my finger and it landed on a mountain with the same name that I had been hearing in my spirit for a good while. I was overwhelmed and excited to know that God was directing me. The next question in my mind was when and how. Putting the thought aside I prepared to go on to the music venue.

When I arrived the coordinator introduced me to a well-known, successful music producer and a couple of male singer-songwriters. One was wearing a white cowboy hat and a fringed jacket and boots. I was impressed and drawn to him. I didn't know any real cowboys especially ones that wrote songs. From the moment we met it was as if we had known each other for a long time. There was such a spiritual connection that I felt from the beginning that we would be best friends. As it turned out both men had homes on the same mountain that God had directed me too. I stood amazed. Both are great singers and songwriters and all around good people. I have written with both of them and one is now my co-writer and duet partner. He lives in another state but comes up to the mountain every few weeks. We have produced a music show together. We started a music magazine and are co-owners of a promotions company. In addition we have a music publishing company. We are excited to see where God will lead us. He is in control and we are trying to let Him guide which is still hard for both of us. We are both independent beings that like to take control but we work very well together and we are trusting God in our ventures. I couldn't have a better partner that I trust more and get along with as well.

We feel that God is leading us to a project that is so big that we won't even attempt to move on it by ourselves. It could benefit many thousands of people. We are waiting for specific direction. If it comes together then we know it is His and if not then we are not concerned because we know that we are not equipped to do it either way. It is fully in His hands.

Decades ago I had such a burden to pray for entertainers in the music business especially in Nashville. Since then God has been faithful and led me to so many that have become friends. They are faith and Holy Spirit filled Christians. They are letting Him shine through their careers. As writers and singers we have often been criticized about our songs. We write and sing about real, everyday life and often that opens the door to tell about Jesus because people know that we understand what they are feeling. We are the Church and we should not relegate God to a building.

God will often use scripture to reveal His will for us individually. In the spirit and in our own prayer language we pray in agreement to what He speaks. We don't usually know how we should pray. Holy Spirit knows the will of God and helps us to know His will as we pray.

NIV (Romans 8:26-27) "In the same way, the Spirit helps us in our weakness. We do not know what we ought to pray for but the Spirit Himself intercedes for us through wordless groans and He who searches our hearts knows the mind of the Spirit, because the Spirit intercedes for Gods people in accordance with the will of God".

There have been times in the midst of praying that a particular verse has come to mind and I know that He is guiding me through His Word. I have read over the same scripture many times then suddenly it seems to come alive because He is applying it to me personally. The Bible is not just an old book. It represents our living God. It is truth. Through His Word He will let His will for us be known or confirmed.

NIV (Luke 10:38) Read the story of Mary and Martha and you may get a better understanding of the importance of giving the Lord undivided attention and listening as He teaches you through spending time with Him. Mary was happy to sit at His feet and learn and worship. She had a heart to hear Jesus. I believe He made it clear that His

Presence was more important than striving as Martha did to put her work in first place.

Listening to Gods' council and being obedient is far better than doing our own will and staying in confusion and restless busyness. If we let Him live through us we are free to be who He made us to be. That simply means total surrender acknowledging Him in every area of our life. Even when we do not realize it God is always near. He is available to love, forgive, nurture, guide and protect us at all times.

Gods inspired words are alive therefore they have life giving power.

There are times that I like to go back and read what we call "The Lords' Prayer." I know it by heart but to read it in black and white reiterates its importance.

Even Jesus prayed to Father God and He teaches us how to pray by His example.

The (KJV) is more poetic but I am using the (NIV) here.

"THE LORDS PRAYER"

NIV (Matthew 6:13) OUR FATHER IN HEAVEN HALLOWED BE YOUR NAME, YOUR KINGDOM COME YOUR WILL BE DONE, ON EARTH AS IT IS IN HEAVEN GIVE US THIS DAY OUR DAILY BREAD AND FORGIVE

US OUR DEBTS AS WE ALSO HAVE FORGIVEN OUR DEBTORS AND LEAD US NOT INTO TEMPTATION BUT DELIVER US FROM THE EVIL ONE.

We shouldn't just say it we ought to pray it to Father God thinking of every word and its significance. We should pray in sincerity from the depths of our souls

NIV(Matthew 6:14) "For if you forgive other people when they sin against you your heavenly father will also forgive you."

God knows the details of our lives so when we pray we need to be specific and pray in faith knowing that He will hear our prayers. Sometimes we may not pray because we feel unworthy. We have to remember that He is worthy. When He is living in us then He is worthy of our communication. He knows our every thought and deed anyway. The attitude of our heart is what is important. We don't have to have any particular body stance and the wonderful thing is that we can talk with Him anywhere any time. We don't even have to pray out loud. Our thoughts can be our prayers if we submit them to Him. There is freedom through Jesus and power in His Name. Holy Spirit tells us to pray then be obedient. Scripture has much to say about prayer.

(1 THESSALONIANS 5:17)
PRAY WITHOUT CEASING

This does not mean constant verbal prayer. Keep a prayer on your heart. If your relationship is open and regular with Father God then you will always have instant access to Him therefore pray without ceasing. Prayer is not a ritual that must be performed at certain times. It is staying in touch with Father. God has many facets of His nature and there are many dimensions of prayer. Time spent in His Presence brings intimacy that cannot be duplicated with any formula. He is less than a breath away. It starts with a desire to know Him and His love.

God is an orderly God and there are ways to pray specifically. When we go to Him we go in the name of His Son Jesus. He paid a high price for us giving His life on a rugged cross for us to have this privilege. We are counted sons and daughters of Almighty God when we accept Jesus, our Savior as our sacrifice. When we confess our sins and ask Jesus into our hearts we begin our prayer journey with the Lord. When we are honest and continually get to know Him then we can make Him Lord of our lives. This is a continuing process as we put Him first in each circumstance of our lives. We learn to let Him live through us gradually as we die to ourselves and put Him first.

PRAYER HINDERANCE

Letting Him have control of our thoughts and choosing the right actions is very difficult for most of us. Often our prayers are interrupted. There have been so many times when I have begun to pray that I would suddenly get so sleepy I could hardly concentrate. There are times that our relationship with God will put us as a target for the enemy. He wants to silence our voice. He wants to put or keep us in despair and depression. If he can find a way to do that then we will not be useful to God or be able to live in our calling. This has happened to me so many times and I have allowed it. I have allowed satan the power to put my calling on hold because of procrastination which stole the time that God could have used me in someone's life.

I remember specifically a time that my procrastination stole an opportunity. I had just moved back to my home state and was passing the home of a woman that I grew up knowing. She was on her front porch and I waved. I knew that I should stop but I was pressed for time and told my mother who was with me that we would go back the next day to visit. The lady died that night and I missed an opportunity to spend time with her. God had a reason to remind me to stop but I was too busy with my own agenda.

When you feel that you can't 'get through' then search your heart and find the reason. It will be on our part not on Gods. It may be a direct attack from satan that takes our focus off of righteous living. Sometimes our attitudes are wrong and prayers will not be answered. Consider motives. Sometimes we pray in a self- serving manner because we want our way. I have done this so many times when I wanted my will instead of His will. There are times that we may get our way and be given our will but be assured it will not be the best for our lives. I have had to learn some tough lessons this way. We can't always know why God doesn't answer our prayers when we want or how we want. If we are in right relationship with Him then we must trust that Father knows best and leave situations or requests in His able hands.

(Isaiah 65:24) "And it shall come to pass, that before they call, I will answer and while they are yet speaking, I will hear."

God speaks to us for many reasons and in many ways. Often He wants to comfort or give assurance to us. Mainly, He wants us to know Him. That knowledge alone is astounding to me. To think that the God of the Universe cares for me enough to speak to me personally is awesome.

WISDOM

NIV (James 1:5-6) "If any of you lacks wisdom, you should ask God, who gives generously to all without finding fault and it will be given to you, (6) but when you ask, you must believe and not doubt because the one who doubts is like a wave of the sea, blown and tossed by the wind."

NIV (Proverbs 9:10) "The fear of the Lord is the beginning of wisdom and knowledge of the Holy One is understanding."

If we are truly wise we can see things from Gods' perspective and measure according to truth and righteousness. Without His direction we face worry, fear and many disappointments in our lives. Things would go so much smoother if we relied on Gods' counsel. Reading His inspired words in scripture as well as time spent in prayer gives us direction. So often we fail by making decisions on our own. Actually, this is one area that has always been difficult for me. Though at first I didn't see it as such I know now that it is pride and I have had to confess it as sin more than once. Father God still reminds me not to go ahead of Him but to seek His way.

Even in my everyday mundane decisions I have trouble reading directions for new products. I try to assemble or figure it out on my own. I usually spend more time doing this than if I read the manufactures directions first. My pride and impatience gets in the way.

NIV (Proverbs 13:10) "Pride only breeds quarrels but wisdom is found in those who take advice."

NIV (Proverbs 16:18) 'Pride, destruction, a haughty spirit goes before a fall.'

If we enjoy spiritual intimacy when we follow His guidance we will be walking in His wisdom and knowledge. Things will fall into place as they should and as He wills. True wisdom is described in:

NIV (James 3:17) "But the wisdom that comes from Heaven is first of all pure, then peace loving, considerate, submissive full of mercy and good fruit, impartial and sincere."

Of course this one is very important and one we are careless of is the Prayer of Thanksgiving.

When I was a child I was taught by my Mother to count my blessings and as the song goes to name them one by one. At the age of about five I remember thanking God for the warmth of the sun and beautiful blue skies. A child's simple prayer but it gave me a foundation to never take for granted even the basic things of life. I am thankful for all the little things my mother took the time to instill in me. She laid a strong foundation with little lessons.

(Psalms 100:4) "Enter into His gates with Thanksgiving and into His Courts with Praise. Be Thankful to Him and Bless His Name."

We take so much for granted here in America. God has so richly blessed us in every area of life. His Grace is overwhelming. I am so thankful for being blessed to be born in this great land and better still in an area that is considered to be the Bible belt. I have so many reasons to be thankful to God. Often we tread on His blessings asking for more and more filled by desire and greed. Recently I read an article that really hit home. It was explaining one of the most successful businesses. Storage buildings are big business in America. It said that we in America collect so much and fill storage buildings because of our emptiness. Of course that does not apply to everyone but it is certainly food for thought. We can be a greedy people as a whole. Often we put things above our spiritual life when we live in excess.

(Galatians 5: 16) "I say then: Walk in the spirit and you shall not fulfill the lust of the flesh".

Without His abiding love I would never have been able to get through many of my life experiences. I abide in Him and He abides in me.

When we go through trials and hard times we need to be thankful. We're not thankful for the trials but through the trials for Gods' Mercy endures and His Grace sustains us.

PRAISE

Acknowledge that God is worthy to be praised in His own right. We can't let our feelings determine whether or not we honor Him through Prayer and Praise. Our feelings do not negate His holiness and worthiness to be praised. We are righteous only in Him.

KJV (Psalm 145:17) "The Lord is righteous in all His ways and holy in all His work."

KJV (Psalm 150:2) "Praise Him for His mighty acts; praise Him according to His excellent greatness".

KJV (Hebrews 13:15) "By Him therefore let us offer the sacrifice of praise to God continually, that is the fruit of our lips giving thanks to his name".

Proclaim Him as Ruler, Christ and King. Wherever we go, when He is with us is Holy Ground.

God is Sovereign which means that He is all knowing, all powerful and free to do His will. Our prayers will be powerless when we do not give God the glory that He deserves. He has unlimited power and glorious grace. We can trust Him and rely on Him to be in charge of every situation in our lives. Through our trust we are free to offer adoration and praise. Scripture tells us to praise with our mouth through song.

KJV (Psalms 95:1) "O come, let us sing unto the Lord; Let us make a joyful noise to the rock of our salvation."

SONG

Since I was a child God has used music to speak to me. Often I will hear a new melody in my spirit and then He gives me the message or the lyrics. Other times he lets me hear a song and if I am not paying enough attention I will hear it again and again. Then I realize that the line or verse in the song is the message that I need to hear. We are always in His Presence though we may not be aware that He is with us even in the little things of life. He speaks if only we will hear with an open heart through our spiritual ears. His truth comes through melodies and lyrics of songs and reminds me of the responsibility that a Christian songwriter has to be biblically correct when writing songs. The following song was founded in Praise.

GOD REIGNS

GOD REIGNS AND HIS SON SHINES
GOD REIGNS AND HIS SON SHINES
TODAY FEELS LIKE HEAVEN TO ME

HE'S BEEN WITH YOU FROM THE BEGINNING
HE KNOWS THE PLANS HE HAS FOR YOU
HE'LL GIVE YOU HOPE AND LET YOU PROSPER
HE'LL ALWAYS SEE YOU THROUGH

YOU ARE HIS CHOSEN TREASURE
HOLY TO THE LORD
IF YOU OBEY HIS WORD AND COVENANT

BE TIED WITH HIS THREE CORDS
GOD REIGNS AND HIS SON SHINES
GOD REIGNS AND HIS SON SHINES
TODAY FEELS LIKE HEAVEN TO ME
GOD REIGNS

© 2011 GLENDA VAUGHN BMI
© 2015 OUR DESTINY MUSIC PUBLISHING BMI

God has given me words as a poem or song lyrics as comfort on many occasions. One such time was at the death of my sister's son. He had been sick for a long time and one day a while before his death God gave me the opportunity to talk with him and we prayed together. I asked him if he knew Jesus as Savior and if he knew that he was saved and would go to Heaven someday. He said that he did not but that he wanted to. I asked him to repeat the sinner's prayer. He did and he asked Jesus into his heart that day. Through our many tears he told me that he knew that he was saved. He didn't live long after that. After he went "home" I wrote the following words for Johnny. He always had a gentle, quiet, loving spirit. When he was a little boy he loved the mornings. He could hardly wait to get outside. I remember his reddish hair glistening in the sun and how his eyes sparkled with adventure at the thought of going fishing, which he loved to do. Through these memories and with these words God gave me comfort.

MORNING SONG

IN THE STILLNESS OF EARLY MORNING
AS THE SUN SHINES GENTLY THROUGH
I'M REMINDED OF SUNNY SMILES
AND I ALWAYS THINK OF YOU

AS THE DAY BEGINS UNFOLDING
NEW DISCOVERIES TO BE MADE
I THINK OF ALL YOUR LIFE STILL TEACHES
AND MY SADNESS ALWAYS FADES

SPARKLING RAIN AND GENTLE BREEZES
THEY REMIND ME OF YOU TOO
FOR IN THEM I HEAR YOUR LAUGHTER
JOY COMES RUSHING THROUGH!

THOUGH YOU'VE TAKEN A SHORT JOURNEY
I KNOW IT WAS GOD'S DIVINE PLAN
TO DRAW YOU INTO HIS KINGDOM

THE TAPESTRY OF OUR MASTERS HAND.

God has given me songs of praise also on many occasions. "My Dwelling Place" the song and the title of this book began through a time of praise and worship. Sometimes songs have begun in my prayer language. God told me long ago that I was to praise and worship Him in song. The following is one part of such a song. It is a joy to know that under the shadow of His wings we find safety, comfort and protection.

IN THE SHADOW OF YOUR WINGS
IN THE SHADOW OF YOUR WINGS
I'LL TAKE MY REFUGE
FOR YOU KNOW DEAR LORD
YOU ARE MY HIDING PLACE

CHORUS

THROUGH YOUR LOVE YOU BLED AND DIED
THEN GLORIFIED YOU SAVED ME
YOUR LOVE KNOWS NO BOUNDS
AND YOU FOUND EVEN ME.

THROUGH IT ALL I DO RECALL
YOU'VE KEPT ME SAFELY

FOR I'M SHELTERED IN
THE WARMTH OF YOUR LOVE

CHORUS

THROUGH YOUR LOVE YOU BLED AND DIED
THEN GLORIFIED YOU SAVED ME
YOUR LOVE KNOWS NO BOUNDS
AND YOU FOUND EVEN ME

© 1999 GLENDA VAUGHN BMI
© 2015 OUR DESTINY MUSIC PUBLISHING BMI

A precious girlfriend reminded me of this scripture several years ago and it impacted my life.

NIV (Psalms 91:4) "He will cover you with His feathers and under His wings you will find refuge, His faithfulness will be your shield."

Just as a baby chicken wanders away from the hens protective feathers it is in danger of being attacked. There may be a predator nearby. Danger is outside its mothers' protection. It may have walked away because it wanted to explore its surroundings. The metaphor is so simple yet God likens it to us. When we stray away from God through our rebellion which is a witchcraft spirit we are out from under his protection. It is our willful choice and there are consequences. Through the cross He offered us safety. We can find protection under the shadow of the cross because Jesus is our protector like a hen that covers her chicks with her wings.

NIV (Matthew 23:37) "Jerusalem, Jerusalem," you will kill the prophets and stone those sent to you, how often I have longed to gather your children together as a hen gathers her chicks under her wings and you were not willing."

The song and this scripture verse remind me that I am protected and cared for and I have every reason to thank God. I will sing Praises to Him for Who He is ! He is worthy to be Praised.

When we enter into his courts with praise, music helps to take us there. When we worship music is not essential but when we offer our voice and music to Him it becomes a part of our worship. Music is how my soul speaks.

We are to praise with our hands. KJV (Psalms 47:1) O clap your hands all ye people, shout unto God with the voice of triumph.

KJV (Psalms 134;2) "Lift up your hands in the sanctuary and bless the Lord".

I have so many reasons to praise and to thank Him. He has blessed me with a loving family, restored health for me and my loved ones. More than that salvation has been given to me and for many of my family. The rest will be saved because He promised and I believe.

NIV (Joshua 24:15) But "as for me and my household we will serve the Lord."

This scripture was on a placard that my husband brought home when we first married. He didn't realize the significance of the promise at the time. It has been dear to me and an encouragement that I've held on to for all these years. Though the placard is chipped and slightly broken it is significant enough to keep.

DARKNESS REIGNED

As much as I have been blessed there have also been Spiritual challenges for me and my family. I will relate only a few incidents that will hopefully give some insight. If these things had not happened to us I might not have believed them. I will not concentrate on the bad things because God brought me and my family through some terrible times. I do not intend to give satan any glory by sharing these experiences. God used these situations to teach me and make us stronger and more aware of whom the enemy is. For that and so many other things I do thank Him.

When my older son was a baby we moved to my hometown. I thought that a small town would be a safer place to raise the children. My husband was ready to retire from his job and wanted a change. I knew the small town had always been a good, safe environment with great schools and we would also be close to family. In early summer we moved as soon as school was out in Atlanta. By then God was allowing me to spiritually discern some things.

Glenda Vaughn

The children and I moved while my husband went back to Atlanta to work out his retirement which was three months away. We wanted to be settled before the new school year began.

We moved into a lovely neighborhood and when he returned three months later we stayed there for almost a year.

Life was pleasant and we all liked being in a small town and enjoyed being with my close knit family. When my second son was on the way we needed more space so planned to move again. My husband found a house and decided to lease it without my seeing it first. With three children and a baby on the way he thought it would be simpler if he took care of it for me.

Though I did appreciate his reasoning I regretted his decision when I walked up on the front steps. There was a real presence there that was absolute evil. The hair on my neck literally stood up and I got chills in the month of August. I couldn't explain it to him but just said that I didn't want to live there. He said he thought that I would like it being so close to the school and that he had already signed a lease. To say that the house was haunted would be laughable by most peoples' estimation.

When God gives one a spirit of discernment it is a blessing that sometimes feels like a curse in some ways. This was the case. It was no laughing matter. What many people call ghosts are in my reasoning evil, demonic spirits. The house was so demon possessed that it was like living a horror movie after a while. Our lives have forever changed. That was over twenty years ago and for years every day was a spiritual battle. My husband changed dramatically. Whatever problems that he had before were multiplied many times over. He began to exhibit more than one personality. Satan did manifest himself in my family during that time in many ways. Almost every night was a nightmare. We all were deeply affected and it took years before my husband saw the light. For those who have never seen Satan's manifestations then you may not understand. It is very real and very dangerous. It takes God's protection and using our Godly authority to fight such evil. The longer we know the Lord however we realize that satan has no more control than what we allow.

One evening my husband came home from work in what I thought was another bad mood. This time was different and as he went into an uncontrolled rage he started choking me. A low, guttural voice said, "I'm going to kill you". It sounded nothing like my husband's voice even when he was angry. His crystal blue eyes were a stormy gray and penetrating. It was as if he were looking into my soul. I was staring into the face of a terrifying enemy. His whole countenance changed before my eyes.

As bad as things had been, I had never encountered this particular malevolent presence in him. I was losing consciousness and all I could whisper was "in JESUS NAME, turn me loose.

He immediately dropped his hands and wanted to know what was wrong with me. He was not speaking in that awful voice anymore either. He denied ever choking or threatening me. There is power in the name of Jesus and demons have to flee. I truly believe that he had no memory of it. There is something about that name that brings peace.

The whole episode was less than five minutes. That convinced me that Satan had taken him over and that was only one of many experiences.

Unless you believe there are demon spirits you will not understand or be aware that these spiritual entities are around every day. They deceive, corrupt and enslave their victims. They do it through alcohol, drugs, sex, envy, gluttony and so many other vices. They torment with self-pity, lack of confidence, bullying, rejection, failure and depression, shame and doubt. They defile through rape, incest, pornography and murder and all manner of sin.

The house always seemed to be full of surprises. There was a space in front of the fireplace that seemed to be an invisible circle. It was icy cold with no explanation.

Once while in the living room I started to hear glass breaking. I walked to the French doors of the dining room and watched as dishes fell from the kitchen counter and broke. There was no one in there. The girls were at school and only the baby and I were home and he was asleep. I started to question my own sanity and knew there was no one that I could tell that would understand. My Baptist family loved me I knew but would never believe that those things were happening. I tried to make excuses to myself saying that there had to be some explanation though I knew in my heart the demon that was facing me. All I knew to do was pray that God would protect us and prepare for a spiritual battle that I did not feel equipped to handle alone. At the time I was not strong at taking authority over demon spirits

I remembered a dream that I had before we left Georgia. It was about a physical fight between me and Satan. I remembered details of the dream but I had no idea what it all meant. God intervened every time and won the fight. If I had been more knowledgeable then I would have known that Jesus would fight this battle for me as well. Ultimately He did but He was teaching me to rely on Him and only Him could I trust.

KJV (Ephesians 6:12) "For we wrestle not against flesh and blood, but against principalities, against powers, against the rulers of the darkness of this world, against spiritual wickedness in high places."

Another incident involved my daughters' doll. She had wanted a Charlie Mac doll and when she received it she spent hours playing. I started to notice that at night she would put it in the corner in the hallway. This went on for a few days when I finally asked her why. She just said that she felt funny when it was in their room. I left it in the hall but after a few times passing it I started to feel a presence in the doll. We all wanted it gone so she gave it to a teacher that collected that kind of doll.

At the time I did not know that demons would inhabit inanimate objects. If I had we would have destroyed it. I really regretted passing it on to someone else. The little that I did know about demons I had learned while attending the full gospel church in Atlanta. Being sensitive to spiritual matters I never sought to know more about them at that time. I was armed with little knowledge but with Gods' guidance and protection we survived living there until the lease was up.

Before we moved from that house our second son was born. The doctors had said that I would not have another child before my first son was born. God proved them wrong. We had a double blessing to have two little boys in two and a half years. This one weighed in at almost ten pounds too and seemed happy and healthy. When we brought him home I laid him in his crib in my bedroom. Almost immediately he started to cough.

My husband was working odd hours and leaving very early in the morning so he slept down the hall. One night my baby started to choke. He was asleep so I immediately got up to check him. He was fine so I got back into bed. It happened again and I felt a frightening presence by his crib. I got back up and put him in bed with me.

I was praying fervently. A few minutes later a figure was standing in my doorway. I thought it was my husband so I spoke to him asking why he was just standing there. "It" never did anything but vanish when I got to the door. I ran down the hall and there was my husband fast asleep. He had to leave before dawn so I didn't wake him. I stayed awake praying and binding spirits. The only thing I knew to say was in Jesus name you are bound and must leave and pled the blood of Jesus over my family.

Later when I did tell my husband he thought that I was hallucinating. I thought that I was totally alone in this battle but God was the One I needed and He was with me. When my baby son was nine months old he began to have seizures. I had taken him to the doctor earlier that day for bronchitis. He was on antibiotics and had only a slight fever. We did not know what was happening to him as he began convulsing. We were terrified. I was on the phone trying to get an ambulance and at the same time praying.

Before the paramedics and police arrived my baby was lifeless and blue. His mouth was no longer shut and his Dad tried to resuscitate him by mouth.

As the policeman got to the door I thrust him into the arms of the officer. Ryan took a faint breath and the policeman started mouth to mouth breathing and worked on him until the ambulance arrived. The paramedics took over and checked him before transporting him to hospital. I thought the night air had forced him to take a small breath but someone said later that it was removing him from the house. God had spared our baby and how He did it was His decision.

Though I do not believe that Christians can be possessed by Satan I do believe that we can be attacked by demon spirits and some say one can be inhabited but not possessed. I know my experiences are real and the name of JESUS can make demons go away. Our attacks did not stop then but Father was always protecting and teaching me through those times. We build strength when we exercise and work at it and those trials were a spiritual workout that made me stronger in faith and trust in God.

Our son stayed in the hospital for a week before being sent home. We thought that the nightmare was over when he had another seizure. My sister Pat had come over to watch him and let us get some sleep. As soon as I got settled in bed she screamed for me to come to them. He was overcome with severe convulsions and he had white foam around his mouth. She tried to hold him but the seizures were so severe she laid him down. Again I called the ambulance. As the policeman came in he immediately turned my baby upside down and hit his back. He was choking on phlegm. The policeman massaged him until his breathing was normal and his color returned. We went back to the hospital where he spent another six days. He was then transferred to a large hospital fifty miles away. He stayed there for another week. He continued to have grand-mal type seizures that would lift his flailing body from the bed as he lost consciousness. It took almost another week of trying to regulate medications until the seizures stopped. He went through extensive tests to rule out a brain tumor. He had E e g s to check brain wave patterns and thankfully had no brain damage from the seizures.

Again God was there protecting him. I watched in fear and helplessness as other mothers on the floor prepared to give their children up. Many had as many as fifty seizures a night because of brain tumors and cancer. All I could do was pray for them and thank God that my sons' tests showed no tumor. We were sent home with a diagnosis of epilepsy. A few months after bringing him home from the hospital we moved from that horrible house.

He stayed on medication until kindergarten. When he had the usual childhood vaccines often he would start the seizures again. The doctor decided that he was allergic to the pertussis in the DPT vaccine which affected him the worst. At that time the pediatrician wanted to add another medication to the one that he was on. He had always been a bright child and he learned quickly. I hated seeing him miss so much and knew the meds and seizures would affect his learning and be especially hard for him when he started to school. After much prayer I believed that God was saying to take him off the medication and trust Him. I told the doctor my decision. He thought it was a mistake but said if I was determined to remove meds to do it gradually. Under his watchful eye we cut the drugs down and after a couple of weeks he was off all medication. I trusted God to take over and as usual He did. My son never had another grand-mal seizure. When he went through puberty he would just have a few seconds of inattention and that was the only after effect. The doctor had said that when he went through hormone changes that he might have those blank outs for a few seconds. Many people have the blank stares for usually less than ten seconds and sometimes it is mistaken for daydreaming.

My son is now grown with a family of his own and successful in business. God restored what satan tried to take away. I am blessed now with seeing his son grow and having a beautiful daughter-in-law that I love as well. God is so good.

NIV (1 Corinthians 1:9) "God is faithful, who has called you into fellowship with His Son Jesus Christ our Lord."

After we moved health problems plagued me for years. I was in pain almost constantly. I saw several doctors and took many medications that helped only for a little while. I was beginning to believe that we had moved all the demons with us.

The strain on my family was terrible and my husbands' stress was escalating. In the midst of my sickness he had to have a tumor removed from his throat. Thankfully it was not malignant as the doctor had predicted that it would be before surgery. As soon as he was home from the hospital my youngest daughter had surgery. We were drowning in medical bills. My husband worked long and hard and savings were depleted to cover medical costs. Satan always seemed to be at the door. Whenever we were blessed some bad circumstance would take it away.

This may be a good time to remind us that it is better to live under the covering of Christ. My husband was not a believer and was not open to my tithing. I strongly believe in tithing. Many women find themselves under these circumstances. We want to be obedient to Christ but when our husbands are not in right order we have a hard time in this area. I needed to find a way to help with finances so I went to work in an office for a while. It took a while but eventually I saved enough to open a daycare center. It also gave me an opportunity to tithe. I learned that the seed we sow can create new tomorrows for God is faithful to bless and multiply what we plant (give) with an open hand. God is our source but He gives us opportunities to help ourselves.

I was still in so much pain it was hard to work. I was treated for symptoms and it took years before a doctor found the root cause. Things improved for about a year when I became very ill again and had to have major surgery. I had several tumors and each one was in some stage of change with cancer cells.

HEAVENLY PLACES

I have had nine surgeries, six miscarriages and four live births. Both feet have been broken and both arms have been broken one of them twice. One of the discs in my neck was broken and had to be fused. Now I have another ruptured disc. I have known pain all too well. As many times as I have been put to sleep for surgery I have never dreamed during a procedure. I'm sure the experience during that surgery was not a dream either. Whatever happened whether I died or not during that time has never been important to me. I never asked the doctor. Granted, he probably would not have believed me if I had told him what happened.

Scripture says to be absent from the body is to be present with the Lord. I was in His presence.

I remember walking and coming to a small dark space, a small divide. It seemed to be about two feet wide and I just stepped over it onto a long road that was like glass. It looked as if it were lighted from underneath. It was glistening and sparkling like liquid gold. The road seemed to be enclosed on either side by what appeared to be glass. The darkness was outside the walls. I was alone but sensed that I was walking toward a peaceful Presence. I could hear my youngest daughter saying, "Mama don't go." "Mama don't go." I could also hear my Mother calling, "Glenda come back." I never turned around. I couldn't seem to stop and was totally focused on what was ahead. I kept walking until I entered a room outside of God's throne room. Everything was bright like many suns shining all around. The light was so incredible. I could see into the throne room but only the bottom portion of Gods' throne was visible. The light was so bright that I could not see His Face. It was such a peaceful place. I wanted to stay but I wanted to be with my family also. It was as if God were letting me decide if I stayed or went back. God was conversing with me but no words were audibly spoken. We were communicating mentally or spiritually. The words that I heard have stayed with me all these years. He said, "You can go back but you can't stay for long." It has been over twenty years so apparently my concept of time is different from His. I have never doubted this experience.

It may sound insane or like a dream but all I know is that it was a "living experience". Heaven was alive with the purest gold and light that I have ever seen. Peace was almost tangible. Communication was love in the sweetest sense. My senses were so heightened. It was a while before

I shared this experience with anyone. Like a young love, I wanted to savor it and keep it close.

Eventually, I did share with a few friends. They just laughed and said that I must have had some really good drugs before surgery. They were so wrong. It was real and I've been homesick for heaven ever since then. There is no fear. Regret would come only from leaving my family and friends. It was a sacred experience that still gives me comfort and peace.

OVERCOMING GRACE

After the surgery I had more employees running the center while I recovered. With all the extra expense it was no longer profitable. Employment in the town was down so I was directly hit by the recession. Eventually I closed the business. After another year in a tumultuous marriage it became clear that something had to change. I have always believed that a marriage commitment should be honored and every avenue of reconciliation should be examined before seeking divorce. I had fought hard to keep our marriage together but it takes partnership to make a marriage work. After much prayer and soul searching I took my four children and moved out. Divorce was not my goal.

Finding peaceful surroundings for me and my children took priority. Finding an outside job with four children was not financially feasible. Also, my children had to come first. I did what I could do at home which was having licensed daycare for six children. Things were going well and my husband visited the children, brought child support without my asking and came over and did the yard work keeping the grass cut without my asking or expecting him to. There were times when he would pick up utility bills and pay them if he saw them out. In many ways he was so good. His controlling temper and abuse was his counterpart and something I refused to accept any longer.

My companion on a daily basis was God. When I think of those times I am always reminded that I cannot live successfully outside the Presence of Jesus. He was with me through it all.

Winter came and brought with it a severe ice storm. I fell on the sidewalk which was covered with ice and tore all the ligaments and tendons from around my knee. The closest orthopedic doctor was an hour away and we had six inches of snow on top of the ice. I was taken to a local hospital but the only thing the emergency room doctor could do was put my leg in a stabilizer until the weather cleared. There was no surgeon available in that tiny town. I was in agony for two days before my sweet nephew braved the bad roads and drove me to an orthopedic doctor an hour away. The horror of it all was that he was driving a small Volkswagen. Ice and snow was everywhere. He took me to an orthopedic doctor who put my leg in a cast. It was not broken and he chose not to do surgery at that time. We went back down the highway almost fifty miles on prayer. Where the ice and snow had melted from the road it had refrozen by the time we left the doctors' office. Often the car was going completely sideways. At one point he lost control and we left the road. When we got stopped we were about a foot from a power pole but no crash. The pole was right next to me. God had spared our life. It was as if we were in slow motion waiting for the inevitable. It was such a soft stop that surely there were angels around. He was able to just drive right back onto the road with seemingly no problem. We managed to get home without further incident which was about another twenty miles.

My husband had come to care for the children and he kept saying that I had to go back home now. He didn't think that I could handle things since I was hurt. I was not going to go under those circumstances. There had to be a better reason. After five days the pain in my leg was almost unbearable and it was severely swollen. I cut the cast off with a butcher knife. We had more snow and it took another two days before my sister could drive the fifty miles to take me to the doctor. By then I could hardly breathe and was hospitalized with blood clots. After two weeks of blood thinners I was taken to another doctor in another town. Finally this orthopedic surgeon operated and I had some relief. All the tendons, muscles and ligaments were torn and only one muscle was attached. It had been so long with terrible care that it was a slow recovery.

I went home with a wheelchair. I had my four children at home and went back to keeping six other children in my home daycare. Looking back I know that God had to give me strength to handle it all. One of the children was a six week old baby. I managed just fine from my wheelchair and all the parents felt confident that their children would be taken care of and they were. I'm not sure that I would have felt the same in retrospect. It was a happy day when I graduated to a walker. From there I went to crutches.

After four months I was recovered and began to think of opening a small business because I knew I needed to earn more money. I had my business plan all worked out. I had saved a little and borrowed a small amount so I opened a deli. There was not one in town so I had no competition. I offered catering too and hired a lady to do wedding cakes as a sideline. After a week my books were full of catering dates and my business was booming.

On Tuesday I had an appointment to get insurance. On Monday night the business burned to the ground. Apparently lightning had hit the building next door and there was no fire wall. I lost everything. It was like a death and I had nothing left and very little desire to keep trying. I cried for days and hope seemed to be a thing of the past.

Again my husband encouraged me to come home. Still it wasn't for the right reason so I wouldn't go. I was struggling financially and after a couple of weeks started babysitting again. I waited three more months before I agreed to try reconciliation. All the promises that he made to me sounded so good. We moved back home and the peace lasted for two weeks.

The same behavior started all over again. By then I had all but given up. If it had not been for my relationship with the Lord I wouldn't have survived. God was faithful. Through the years there seemed to be one struggle after another.

There came a time that I was having trouble lifting my leg. This would go on for a couple of weeks then it seemed fine. Usually in about two months the same thing would happen again. This went on for half a year before I had tests. No one could tell me what the problem was. By this time I had to drag my leg I couldn't lift it at all.

I saw a neurologist then and he scheduled a spinal tap. My Mom was due to have open heart surgery that day but I was assured that my spinal tap would be over in plenty of time. Things did not go as planned and my spinal fluid leaked out. I couldn't lift my head at all so blood was taken from my arm and injected into my spine to raise the volume. Nothing ever seemed to go smoothly. My Mother was already in surgery when I got to her hospital and I was in so much pain that I could hardly be still. During the night she coded and then was resuscitated. She was rushed back to surgery and was in critical condition.

We had wonderful doctors that God used to save her on several occasions. Each time there was crisis they prayed for her and us and prayed with us. Each time they said they had done all that they could. It was up to God. That is when she would make incredible strides toward recovery though she was in hospital for three months.

During that period my test results came back and the diagnosis was progressive Multiple Sclerosis. The doctor said that I would be in a wheelchair permanently within five years. I said no. I don't accept that. God has always been faithful and He has other plans. I have been through years of pain but not another wheelchair for me and no M S. I am thankful to God for His touch. My brother has had MS for years. With Gods mercy and grace I have overcome that prognosis. My Mother went on to live another fifteen years and with Gods healing overcame an early death. Soon I had a problem with my leg again. A tumor had developed inside my knee so the doctor went in to take it out but didn't remove it. He wouldn't risk cutting it away from all the muscle that it was entwined with.

So much had happened for so long that I literally just wanted time alone to regenerate. I wanted to spend time with God in prayer and to study His word. I was hungry for His Presence. Being knocked off my feet physically was not what I had in mind. It did give me the time that I needed though. I spent hours daily praying, reading His Word and listening to Him.

One day after praying I started to smell the fragrance of roses. It was so sweet and so strong. Jesus Himself seemed to be standing by my closet door. I could feel His Presence and He seemed close enough to touch. A few nights later I woke myself praying out loud in my prayer language. There was a scripture verse on my mind as I opened my eyes. I didn't remember having read it before so I got up and read:

NIV (Isaiah 54:5) "For your Maker is your husband; the Lord Almighty is His name, the Holy One of Israel is your Redeemer; He is called The God of all the earth."

NIV (Isaiah 54;6) "The Lord will call you back as if you were a wife deserted and distressed in spirit- a wife who marries young only to be rejected says your God." It spoke directly to my heart.

A few nights later I was praying for my husband. I felt very burdened for him and had to intercede. He was especially difficult that week. Finally about two in the morning I felt at peace. God had given me a promise through scripture. I could finally sleep. The next morning about nine o'clock there was a knock at the door. A lady that I did not know was at my door asking to talk with me. She said that she was on her way to her church for a meeting when God told her to come and give me a message. She shared the same scripture that God had given me at two in the morning. It was a promise. He was just reiterating it through her. We prayed and she went on her way. We did not know each other at all before then. My husband would be saved. That was the promise. I knew that God was in control and I knew that I could believe it. He just confirmed it through a stranger.

However, I didn't know how long it would take or what the circumstances would be. When I was better I went to work at a radio station with an hour and a half commute. Both of our daughters had gotten married within six weeks of each other and both of the boys were in college out of town. I had decided to finally get my college degree when my husband lost his job three months before his second retirement. He had always worked and couldn't just retire. He lost most of his retirement money also. He became very depressed and started talking about suicide. He refused to see a secular counselor or a church counselor. Many days when I went to work he would say that he wouldn't be there when I returned. I missed a lot of work not knowing what to do. Finally he agreed to see a doctor and was hospitalized for a week. He was supposed to stay two weeks for evaluation but he checked himself out after a week. The doctors prescribed heavy anti-depressants. His former boss came to visit and he prayed to receive Jesus. I would like to say things changed for the good permanently but it was short lived. His previous behavior started all over again. This time I knew that I would die at his hands if I stayed. I had prayed for years and I finally had to totally surrender him to the Lord one last time. That is when I moved out.

I continued to check on him making sure that he had what he needed, cooking meals and taking them over and taking him to doctor appointments We were separated for six years before I filed for divorce though I never stopped praying for him. It was not a decision that I took lightly because I never had wanted it to come to a family break up. I prayed for a long time before making it and when I felt peace then I knew it was the right decision. Actually I felt that I had been released from this marriage. There was regret but no guilt.

Later he developed an inoperable brain aneurysm. I went with him to the neurologist who said it would take a miracle for him to live. That is when he truly repented and asked for Gods help. Within a short time he said he felt that he was healed. We went back to the neurologist who did tests and confirmed that he had indeed had a miracle. I saw the scans before and after and it truly was a miracle. I trust this major Hospital and their doctors. He had a wonderful, praying physician. I have seen the change and I know that he is healed and best of all he is saved. I can also tell from the fruits of the Spirit. He is kinder, more thoughtful and looks for ways to help others. He is concerned for others salvation and witnesses often. This was another prayer answered though it took years to come to pass. God is faithful and He was ready but we all have to be surrendered.

TREASURES IN EARTHEN VESSELS

For many years God has spoken to me in dreams and once I had a true vision that came to pass. One afternoon I sat on the bed to rest. Suddenly I was seeing an older lady with very distinctive features. I felt an overwhelming urgency to pray for her immediately. I had never had this happen when I was fully awake. I remember saying God this must be You and I trust that this lady is real and not my imagination. I went on to pray in the spirit for her until I felt a sense of release. A few months later I was in a shopping mall in Decatur, Alabama when I walked face to face with the woman. I didn't feel a need to speak with her though she hesitated briefly before walking on, as if she knew me. I believe that God orchestrated that meeting to show me that she was indeed real and that it was Him that spoke to me. I've often wondered what He might have said to her. I may never know the value of that moment but the memory is etched in my mind and heart.

When we know Gods love and rest in His love then we can be free to be and do what He calls us into. There are times when God gives me the same dream three times. It has happened many times. He gave me such a dream and then after much prayer He told me what it meant. I dreamed that I was finding treasured pots that were hidden in various places. Some were behind walls in old, dilapidated houses. Some were lost in fields and some in barns and in the attics of beautiful mansions with winding staircases. Every time that I looked for the ones in attics there was always a scary, sinister feeling and I was very frightened.

I recovered all kinds of pots and vases. Some were chipped. Some were broken and others were dirty with hairline fractures. Though they were marred by time and discarded I could tell that they were of great value. Each was unique and beautiful in its own way. I brought all of them home, washed and cleaned them one by one then displayed them on a riser in the sun. When they were sparkling clean and dry I took them inside my home. They were so colorful and decorative, all exquisitely crafted. For the first time sunlight filled the room where I placed them. Some were small, others large, all shapes, sizes and colors.

I prayed for God to show me what this dream meant since I had dreamed it three times. He told me that these Vessels were women that had been broken and hurt. They had to be rescued, healed and shown how beautiful they were regardless of size, shape and color. That was my job to encourage and help restore women that had been hurt like I had been.

The times that I felt fear when going to the attic spaces was because of a strongman spirit over some of them. I had to identify and overcome that spirit to release them. I was to lead them to Him the true restorer.

These vessels had to be mended and made ready to be filled with the Holy Spirit so that they could be used.

I know that I have not yet reached all the women that I am supposed to help. At one time when I was sick and felt that I should be ministering to other women I told God that if that was what He wanted then He would have to bring them to me. I was willing but couldn't go to them.

Within a couple of hours my phone started to ring and many women in town wanted to come over and pray about different situations that they were facing. The ones that could not come to me I prayed with over the phone. This continued for months and I was blessed to have their trust and to know Almighty God was listening to all of us. Everyone's need is significant to our Heavenly Father. Was I ever surprised! I was thinking someday. He was saying that day.

HOLINESS

If we are to be totally submitted to God to be used for His purpose and glory then we must strive to walk in holiness. I have a long way to go to get to the place of holiness that God requires of each of us. I have put Him aside so many times but His Mercy stays with me. We should crave His Presence because that is where holiness is found and being with Him will change us to become more like Him. There are many scripture verses that lead and encourage us to seek a life of holiness.

Once I visited a church where Evangelist Jesse Duplantis was preaching. The spirit was so strong that it felt like a wind was blowing and I literally had to hold to the back of the bench in front of me. I was in the back of the church. Several went up for prayer including me because he had a word to speak over us. He was starting to prophesy over me and when he spoke and pointed to my head it was like a bolt of electricity hit me. I was down for the count and I had no control over my knees buckling. That was powerful and I knew I had met a man that spent time in God's Presence. That was holiness in action.

Scripture tells us that whoever truly loves God and keeps His commands will be loved by God the Father and Jesus the Son and that Jesus would manifest Himself to them. (John 14:21)

My sisters and I decided to take my Mother to a service while Jesse was in town. She had suffered from diabetes for years and I felt sure that God would heal her that night. Jesse came over to our side of the church and said God is healing someone in this area from diabetes. I truly felt it was my Mama. I told her that I thought it was her and to accept the healing. She was a Godly woman but did not seem to believe it was for her. When she went home she continued to take her insulin and became extremely ill over the next few days. I can't prove it as fact but I believe that she was healed of diabetes that night and the insulin made her sick because she didn't need it. We have to know how to accept the gifts that God gives. I believe that too was a mark of holiness because Jesse was submitted to whatever God wanted to do. Jesus was manifest that night.

NIV (1 Peter 1:14-16) "As obedient children, do not conform to the evil desires you had when you lived in ignorance. But just as He who called you is holy, so be holy in all you do, for it is written Be holy, because I am holy."

(2 Corinthians 7:1) "Therefore, since we have these promises, dear friends let us purify ourselves from everything that contaminates body and spirit perfecting holiness out of reverence for God."

I have had many experiences where God has used visiting evangelists to speak into my life. I believe that God gives people 'words of knowledge' and I am confident of the ones that gave these particular words to me. I knew them to be true because they were a witness in my spirit. Once a lady prophet from Mississippi came to my church and spoke words of knowledge to many people that night. I was one of them. We didn't know each other at all.

Before she prayed she said that she was seeing words, a string of words and she didn't understand but she went on to tell me what God said to her. She told me that she could see me standing on the edge of a cliff and the words were my ladder to the other side. As a writer and lover of words I knew what God was saying to me through her.

Another time a well -known evangelist from Birmingham, Alabama came to our church to preach a revival. In the midst of his sermon he started to cry and started walking toward the middle of the church where I was. He got down on his knees and said to me, "please forgive me on behalf of all the men that have hurt you from the time you were a little girl". He said for me not to try to remember. I didn't want to remember more. We did not know each other and he knew nothing of my circumstances past or present. I had never told anyone anything about two instances that had happened to me as a child. I could remember only a few details. I remembered the pain but I didn't know why. The name of one of my daddy's friends kept coming to my memory year after year but I didn't know why. Only Holy Spirit could have let him know those things. I knew that he was a man of integrity and had a close walk with God and it all resonated in my spirit.

ENTERTAINING ANGELS

From the time that I was a small child I have had the privilege of seeing angels. I have no idea why but I have known their presence on several occasions. I probably kept them busy while growing up. When my Granddaddy died I was about seven years old. My Daddy, my aunt and uncle had been with him and came home soon after. I had been up to go to the bathroom when up in the corner of the hallway I saw an angel. I couldn't tell time but somehow knew that it was five in the morning. Later when they came home they said my Papa had died at five in the morning. I never knew the significance of seeing the angel or why I was allowed to or why the time mattered. At other times growing up I was aware of their presence and felt safe. Still I have to wonder where they were when I was a child and was hurt. Why didn't God send them to protect me then?

The Bible has much to say about angels and obviously the created beings are important to God and useful to us. They have the power to perform work for God that is beyond our human ability and strength. When the apostles were jailed by the Sadducees God sent angels to open the door of the prison

NIV (Acts 5:19 says) 'but during the night an angel of the Lord opened the doors of the jail and brought them out.'

Angels are Gods messengers and are sent to minister and protect Gods children.

Another time I was really hurting and very depressed. I felt that I was totally alone without a friend in the world. My girls were married and lived in different towns. My husband had taken our sons out of town to visit his family and I was left alone. I literally just needed a hug when I physically felt that I was being held and hugged. No one was there so who else would it be? I thought it must have been an angel. It doesn't matter if anyone agrees with that supposition. It was comforting to me and what I needed at the time. God knew.

Once on a trip to Birmingham with my Mom and two sisters we encountered who we all felt to be an angel. A truck was in front of us and was loaded with pieces of metal. Things started to fall off the truck and several people including us were going from lane to lane to keep from being hit from falling debris. We were all dodging traffic as well. Suddenly we had run over a small item and got a flat tire. My sister managed to get off the freeway without incident which is no easy task in morning traffic. Somehow she was able to drive right off the road onto a secondary road. It seemed out of nowhere that there was a utility truck that came right to us. Three men changed the tire and we never missed our Mother's doctor appointment. We were convinced that one of the men was an angel. There was such a kindness in his eyes and peace emanated from him. We could feel the peace from yards away.

Another experience was when I was in a candle lit prayer service in my church. It was one of those times when we could come and pray quietly and leave whenever we wanted. I was sitting on a back row alone when I felt someone touch my shoulder. I turned but no one was there. It happened again and then the third time I turned around quickly and saw an angel that appeared to be about ten feet tall. He was gone as soon as I recognized that he was an angel. That was on a Friday night.

On Sunday I went to early evening service at church and suddenly got sick as the service was beginning. I had reached the side door where the usher was standing when I became very weak and felt faint. The usher gave me a chair and the Pastor came back to see me. He prayed for me and asked if I knew that my Guardian angel was behind me. I didn't see him but I told the pastor that I had seen him on Friday night. He agreed that he seemed to be about ten feet tall. Again I don't know why I was allowed to see him. I think it was that the Lord was letting me know that (HIS Goodness and Mercy) would be with me all my life.

(Psalm 23:6) "Surely goodness and mercy shall follow me all the days of my life and I will dwell in the house of the Lord forever."

There is so much information in scripture concerning angels and their duties. That is a study within itself and something I will not attempt here. We cannot allow ourselves to put our trust in them instead of the Lord. We can't make anything a God over our God Jehovah. Of course there are the ones sent by God but Satan is a counterfeiter and has his fallen angels to do his bidding too.

I believe in asking the Lord to surround my family and friends with His holy angels from heaven to protect and provide for them. Someone may have prayed that prayer for me during my life and perhaps that is why I have been allowed to see them. Since Satan has his host as well I ask specifically for Gods holy angels.

WHO ARE YOU IN CHRIST

Sometimes we want to qualify for heaven as if we ever could on our own. We could never do enough or be good enough to get there. Don't waste time trying to work your way in. The price has been paid in full by the blood of Jesus. As Christians we struggle with our identity sometimes. We may question our salvation though we know we have made a decision to follow Christ. We are not perfect but we just have to ask and accept His forgiveness if we feel that there is something in our way. We also have to remember that there is no condemnation in Christ Jesus. Satan will try to make us carry a load of condemnation because he is the accuser and a liar.

Many of us have stayed in spiritual and emotional prisons for too long. Satan has held the keys because he makes us feel unworthy and we have accepted that. We have to realize whom we belong to and accept that through no work of our own we are sons and daughters of The Living God Jehovah.

Scripture reminds us of who we are if we take the time to read His Word. I am going to share just a few scriptures to reaffirm our identification if there is any question in your minds. We know that God's Word is true. Jesus is Truth and Holy Spirit is Truth.

We need to apply what they say about us so we can live in freedom knowing that because of Jesus we are heirs to Royalty. We are sanctified in Christ to be used for His good purpose as we walk in His Light. His goodness and perfection transforms us and renews our mind. His glory is reflected in our Joy as we stay in His Presence.

The Bible is full of scriptures telling us who we are if we belong to Jesus.

NIV (1 Corinthians 6:19) Do you not know that your bodies are (temples of the Holy Spirit) who is in you, whom you have received from God.

NIV (2 Corinthians 5:20) We are Ambassadors to Christ

NIV (Peter 1:23) We are Gods Children

NIV (Revelation 12:11) We are Over comers

NIV (2 Peter 1:3-4) We are Partakers of His Divine Nature

NIV (James 1:22, 25) We are Doers of The Word

NIV (John 15:15) We are a Friend of Jesus

NIV (Romans 8:2) We are Free from the law of sin and death

NIV (Ephesians 1:4) We are Holy and Blameless in His Sight in Love

These are only a few of the ways that God says that we are in Him. Our uncertainty about life can fill us with turmoil, anxiety and make us fear. If we study the way that God sees us it will help us to be who He has called us to be. We each have gifts and talents and often people will ask me what their gifts are. That is not for me to say but there are a few markers that help each of us to know. Of course spending time with God helps us to know what He is leading us into.

I have found that when we are in Christ we will recognize what our strongest passion is. We all have a creative side because we are fashioned after The Creator. It may be your vocation or not but as long as we submit our gifts and talents to the Lord and ask Him then He will lead us down the right path to use them. We can rest and enjoy the journey knowing that He has our best interest in mind and it will work for His purpose. We all need to quit judging our life's success from a monetary value. Our jobs and our past do not define who we are or who God created us to be. That is not how God judges and it is freeing to know that He is in control if we let Him be.

One of the best markers that I know in making decisions is Gods Peace.

NIV (26:3) 'He will keep us in perfect Peace whose mind is stayed on you.'

When we focus on the love that our Heavenly Father has for us then we know that we can trust Him to guide us by His Peace. Turn away from the fear of making the wrong decisions. Take your thoughts off the circumstance and place them on Gods Goodness. It is such a simple solution but we make life so hard. Rest in Him.

I can never relate all the times that God has shown every part of His Personality to me. He is everything. I wouldn't want to know what my life would be without Him. I am Blessed and Highly Favored. The Lord Jehovah is my God. Jesus Christ, The Risen One is my Redeemer and King and Holy Spirit is my Companion.

Here He lives in me. When I'm gone from this earth I will live with Him eternally. Our souls never die. Life never stops we just live in a different place. Heaven is real and I believe that Hell is real. Since I have seen Heaven there is no fear. If you have not chosen Jesus as your Savior please don't let another day pass by without confessing your sins and asking Jesus to abide in you and you in Him. Glenda Vaughn

ABOUT THE AUTHOR

Glenda Vaughn is blessed to be a mother of two daughters, two sons, five grandchildren, and two great-grandsons. She is a country/gospel singer and songwriter in Nashville, Tennessee and co-owner of Our Destiny Music Publishing, America's Musical Memories Showcase, America's Musical Memories Magazine, and Donovaughn's (Tin Star Media) with duet partner and co-writer Ricky L. Gooden.

Printed in the United States
By Bookmasters